D1407552

SHREVEPORT
LIBRARY

A Historical Perspective

The Red River

Produced by Commercial National Bank
of Shreveport, Louisiana

Moran Publishing Corporation
Baton Rouge, Louisiana

Moran Publishing Corporation
Baton Rouge, Louisiana
Manufactured in the United States of America

Contents

Introduction

The Red River has long played a tremendous and vital role in the history, development and success of North Louisiana. Intertwined like a winding thread with the lives of area residents, the Red River spurred the founding of Shreveport, ushered in the colorful steamboat era and encouraged local economic expansion.

Today, the resplendent red torrent rushes by rejuvenated skylines, past bustling industrial complexes, and under countless bridges. Its waters continue to provide the North Louisiana area with transportation, commerce and recreation. It is a vital link for us all—a major contribution of our heritage, a permanent part of our past, our present and our future.

Because of the river's great importance, we at Commercial National Bank in Shreveport commissioned this book as a public service to tell its story.

The Red River has been instrumental in the growth of this area, but people create that growth. And the growth of Commercial National Bank has been contingent upon the support of you—our friends—and it is to you that we dedicate this tribute to the Red River.

W. WARREN FULLER
President
Commercial National Bank

Big Red

Its Early History

It winds itself like some great rust-colored serpent through five states, traversing a distance of 1,275 miles on its journey. It has throughout the years maintained with the people who inhabit its banks a sort of uneasy truce, serving at once as a source of sustenance and of danger. Filled with a dense red sediment, this whimsical and uncertain river becomes a seasonal tyrant with the onset of heavy rains, periodically churning itself into a swollen, threatening giant. Its history is comprised of a fascinating melange of Indians, Spaniards, Frenchmen and Americans; of massive log jams and picturesque steamboats; of Civil War battles and local duels fought on its shore. It is called Big Red by those who know its temperament and respect its power. It is the Red River.

When Europeans first arrived on the banks of the Red River, they found Indians living in the valley, descendants of prehistoric nomadic tribes dating from 10,000 B.C. These earliest tribes, the Caddo, Coushatta, Kisatchie and Natchitoches Indians, were big game hunters and gatherers who traveled in small bands, following herds of migratory animals along the river's course. Their lifestyle soon gave way to a somewhat more locally confined manner of living, characterized by larger social groups.

The Poverty Point Indians, at the time the most sophisticated culture in America north of Mexico, developed in the period from approximately 1500 B.C. to 1500 A.D. These tribes had become at that point more sedentary than their ancestors, cultivating native plants, and building large earthworks along the banks of the Red.

During the transitional period from the deterioration of the Poverty Point cultures to the arrival of Europeans, the river became more of a direct

Long before the arrival of Europeans along the Red River, the Poverty Point Indians had developed a sophisticated culture centered around an agricultural lifestyle.

source of food and transportation to the Indians. As cultures became more sophisticated, agriculture flourished, cultivation increased, and the utilization of pottery and weapons became commonplace. Whatever else changed in the gradual metamorphosis of the Indians' life, the river remained a constant: unpredictable, often threatening, yet somehow unchanging over the centuries.

The earliest European exploratory efforts centered largely around the Mississippi and the Gulf Coast. In 1542 the Spanish explorer Hernando DeSoto, seeking the Mississippi River, headed an expedition down the Red's meandering course. While he was probably the first European explorer to discover its fertile delta, the Frenchmen René Robert Cavelier Sieur de LaSalle and Henri de Tonti were not far behind.

In 1672 the Governor of Canada heard of the experiences of DeSoto's party and felt a great urge to know more of the Indians and the Mississippi River. He sent out Joliet and Marquette, the "monk and the merchant," to explore further. They returned with wonderful news of their explorations to the mouth of the Arkansas and the Red. This joyful enterprise set the cathedral bells of Canada to "ringing all day long" in celebration.

In spite of these journeys, many of which included territory claimed by the Red as its basin, the Red River Valley remained largely unknown until the 1700s.

In the year 1700, the French explorer Jean Baptiste Lemoyne sur de Bienville traveled up the Red River, leading a retinue of soldiers and Indians, including his kinsman, Louis Juchereau de St. Denis, to determine the extent of the Red River Valley. Traveling toward the area that would later be Shreveport, Bienville found there tribes of friendly Indians, and after a brief survey the expedition returned safely and successfully to its starting point at Biloxi.

Ten years later St. Denis returned, searching for the legendary gold and silver rumored to exist along the Red River, though these metals are not native to its river banks. Despite his failure to find such riches, St. Denis remained in the area, and it was he who founded the town of Natchitoches in 1714.

One year earlier, in 1713, Fort St. Jean Baptiste was established, near the present-day location of Natchitoches. A small trading post, it now bears the distinction of being the oldest permanent settlement in that area of modern Louisiana. Poste due Rapides, a small French garrison, was founded in 1723 across the Red River from the modern site of Alexandria—now Pineville.

The Spanish colonial period marked an influx of immigrants from France, Spain, the Canary Islands, the rest of the United States and Santo Domingo. The Treaty of Fontainbleau, signed in 1762, transferred French territory to Spain. Both the Creole and Acadian peoples who evolved as a result of French and Spanish colonization are testimony to the harmonious blending of diverse cultures that characterizes Louisiana today.

Artist's conception of Fort St. Jean Baptiste, established in 1713

The river, ever-important as a transportation artery to settlers, began to take on larger significance with the development of plantations and the importation of slaves for plantation labor. Cotton and sugar cane reigned as the major agricultural crops, benefiting from the fertile soil built up over the years by the Red's periodic overflows. However, flooding remained a huge problem, as the quixotic river rose and fell with the seasons.

As more and more white settlers poured into the Red River Valley with the change of government, the Indian tribes began a slow exodus from their native banks. Exploited by the white man, especially after the French and Indian War, they were forced to move north, leaving few remnants of what had once been a proud and largely peaceful people.

Secret treaties and international high finance characterized the events surrounding the Louisiana Purchase in 1803. Spain returned Louisiana to French control in November of 1803, with France transferring Louisiana to the United States in December. The cost of this massive purchase of land was an incredible two cents per acre! Permanent settlers, most of them Americans, penetrated the valley. And while most of the early historic events naturally centered around Natchitoches, the oldest settlement, the first event of interest occurring near Shreveport was recorded in 1806.

To establish American presence in the new territory, President Thomas Jefferson's War Department sent out an expedition to survey the area, determining geographic features and boundaries of the Louisiana Purchase. This force was headed by Thomas Freeman, a surveyor, who was to determine geographical positions by astronomical observations, and Dr. Peter Custis, a botanist and natural historian.

The expedition began at Natchitoches in April, 1806, and two months later arrived near the Oklahoma-Texas line. The journey was hazardous, river transportation at the time being somewhat primitive, and largely comprised of keel-boats, rafts, flatboats, pirogues, and French bateaus. Navigation of the river was further complicated by log jams. Because of the impassability of great portions of the water, further attempts at navigation and exploration of the river were thwarted at the time.

The Great Raft, as it became known in the 1830s, began when the Red River's original channel, now the Cane River, was bisected by the Mississippi River at Rackasee Bend. It received waters from the upper channel and dumped its own overload into the amputated lower channel. What is now the Atchafalaya River was formed on the Gulf end of the Red's channel. A wide blockage of driftwood appeared in the river's mouth, in the Mississippi's backwaters. At the shallows, fifty miles up Red River, it formed and began to penetrate upstream, growing at the rate of one mile per year, as additional driftwood lodged against its head.

As the Indians began to move out of the state, the government set aside a reservation for them in Indian Territory (now Oklahoma) in 1830. The establishment of this reservation, coupled with the building of an army post at Fort Townson, at the northern reaches of the river, created a demand for clearing of the Great Raft. The Red River was the logical route to send army supplies to the fort, and the government called upon an experienced river man for the solution to its problem.

In 1833 Captain Henry Miller Shreve laboriously worked his way up-river, mile by mile, calling upon his considerable expertise at transforming impassable rivers into navigable arteries. As the Louisiana Purchase and Red River Valley became more clearly divided into the states of Louisiana, Arkansas, Texas and Oklahoma, the river once again became a center of navigation during high water months. Alexandria, Shreveport, Pineville and Natchitoches experienced rapid growth as river ports for handling increased agricultural production, stimulated by the introduction of the steamboat and prior clearing of the river.

In 1835 the Caddo Indians sold their land to the United States and moved west, presenting opportunities for more extensive settlement by people from other parts of the country. In 1837 the first railroad west of the Mississippi River, the Red River Line, was established. This line connected Cheneyville and Alexandria for the purpose of transporting cotton and sugar to the steamboats on the Red River.

Louisiana seceded from the Union in January, 1861, as the Civil War gained momentum and battle flags were raised. Due to its central location on the river and its modest amount of industrial development, Shreveport served as the Confederate capital of Louisiana. It is said that the Red River campaign in the spring of 1864 undoubtedly helped prolong Confederate resistance during the war.

During the late 1800s and early 1900s, the large scale influx of rail-roads, the western movement of the frontier, and the problem of keeping the Red River open to shipping finally took their toll. Cut off from the river traffic by the slow demise of the sternwheelers and the ebbing flow of water due to flood control measures upstream, Shreveport gradually ceased to be a working waterway. Steamboat and barge traffic decreased and finally disappeared at the beginning of this century.

Physical Characteristics of the River

Imagine yourself in a sternwheeler, sitting squarely in the middle of a rust-colored expanse of river at its headwaters, about to begin an exciting and perilous journey down into the Red River Valley. Beginning in eastern New Mexico, the Red flows meanderingly through the northern Texas panhandle and southern Oklahoma, forming the border for those two states, thence through the southwest tip of Arkansas.

Near Fulton, Arkansas, the river turns south, entering Louisiana at the northwest tip, bisecting the cities of Shreveport and Bossier, as well as Caddo and Bossier parishes. Curving down toward south Louisiana, sixty-five miles north of Baton Rouge along the Mississippi state border, it converges with Old River, which flows directly into the Mississippi River.

Described as a "very whimsical river" by a report for the *New Orleans Crescent* in 1860, the Red passes through lands comprised of alluvial soils rich in iron oxide, giving the water its rusty color and the river its name. It is not, like many less fortunate rivers that have met a twentieth-century fate, polluted.

The river acts as a political boundary for Avoyelles, Bossier, Caddo, Catahoula, Concordia, Grant, Natchitoches, Pointe Coupee, Rapides, Red River and Winn parishes.

A leisurely journey down the Red River in the heyday of the steamboat was, if somewhat hazardous, nonetheless beautiful. The Red River Basin has a drainage area of 69,200 square miles, most of it gently rolling terrain with elevations of less than 400 feet sea level. Only a small portion, within the Ouachita Mountains in the northern part of the basin, is characterized by narrow, steep-sided valleys and ridges.

While certainly less comfortable for travelers in pre-air conditioning days, the climate of most of the basin might be described as mild, with long summers. The days are generally hot and nights moderately warm, with sub-freezing temperatures and snowfall to be occasionally expected during moderate winters. The annual mean temperature is a pleasant sixty-five degrees Fahrenheit.

The riverboat traveler might discern several different types of lush flora throughout the river's valley. The bottomland hardwood and cypress region, including the parishes of Concordia and Avoyelles, as well as the river's flood plains, abounds in vegetation. The longleaf pine region, on either side of the flood plain in Rapides, Grant, Winn and a portion of Natchitoches Parish, is characterized by the denser, taller trees with which northern Louisianians are familiar. The land on either side of the river adjacent to the flood plain through the remainder of the project area bears shortleaf pine, oak and hickory. It is, all in all, a lovely sight for the journeyman, with verdant forests at every bend and along both banks of the river.

The Red River Valley abounds with wildlife, and the sale of both meat and fur from furbearers in Louisiana represents a considerable monetary input into the state economy. Among the native animals living in the valley are nutria, muskrat, beaver, possum, red and gray squirrel, raccoon, mink, otter, skunk, white-tailed deer, swamp rabbit, red and gray fox, and cottontails. Resident game birds include bobwhite, wild turkey and king rail, along with ducks and geese.

Lining the river's levees one can often spot rows of fishermen's shanties, lean-to shacks and frame houses. Using nets and trot lines, these fishermen sell their catch wholesale to the city's groceries and retail to small fish houses and markets. Channel catfish is one popular game fish native to the Red River, as well as shad, shiner, carp, white bass, crappie, bluegill, and blue catfish.

It is through the abundance of such wildlife that the nickname, "Sportsman's Paradise," has been applied to Louisiana. The profusion of such lush vegetation, the proliferation of various types of fauna, and the humid, semi-tropical climate all combine to give this particular portion of the Red River Valley an almost exotic, jungle-like atmosphere.

Historically, the recreation pursuits of persons living within the river's basin have been rural in nature and centered around stream, river and pond fishing and a variety of hunting activities. The predominantly rural, agrarian background of many area residents in tiny villages and towns along the river's banks has encouraged them to prefer these activities. This preference has been intensified by the fact that in the past there have been few facilities available for other outdoor recreation activities.

Minerals produced along the river banks are well-known: petroleum, natural gas, sand, gravel and clay are the most important of these. The surface waters of the Red have been used for public water supply, industrial water supply, fishing, wildlife, plant life, hydropower, agriculture, navigation, waste assimilation, recreation, and esthetics.

In Shreveport, the Red River flows adjacent to the city for approximately two miles. During the steamboat era, the city's economic, and often even social activity centered around the river, with diverse types of businesses growing up along its banks. Before the trunk line railroads were under construction, navigation on the Red River was of great importance, supplying Shreveport and surrounding trades territories with an outlet for cotton and other products.

As the town grew, bridges were built, and the river no longer permanently divided the cities of Shreveport and Bossier (originally called Cane City). Acting in addition as a natural divider between the parishes of Caddo and Bossier, the Red River became in a way a social dividing line; the city of Shreveport, as a major steamboat port and gateway to the western areas, grew rapidly more sophisticated, while Bossier City, at first considered a "suburb" of Shreveport, has only recently come into its own as a full-fledged city.

The Red River has displayed a tendency in the past to swing over to the East, cutting new channels and leaving the old bed. It is this action which created Old River, Bayou Pierre and 12 Mile Bayou. And it is partly this unpredictability of course which has made its prospects with regard to navigation seem rather bleak.

With an average width of 975 feet, the river is 1,275 miles long, with a moderately swift current. Due to its wide banks and wide river bed, however, the current is not of sufficient strength to cut a naturally navigable channel in the river.

After years of disuse, the Red has in some ways become a liability to the people who inhabit its valley. The river has always been characterized by a series of sinuous curves, by wide variations in depth, by shifting beds and banks, and by unpredictable shoaling. In the bends of the river, the eroding action of the current attacks the banks, causing caving to occur. These continually receding banks plague the people living along the river, with the rate of recession depending upon the shape of the bend, the composition and slope of the land, and river stage. Before the present levee system was designed, flooding habitually ruined farms and houses throughout the valley.

As the physical shape of the river has changed somewhat since the time of the Indians, so has its use. From source of food to transportation artery, the Red River has throughout the passage of the years been central to the development of Shreveport. Recent years have seen the restoring of the old riverfront area and the addition of new businesses, restaurants and entertainment ventures within its immediate surroundings. Attempts to reopen the river to major navigation once again have prompted action by the U.S. Army Corps of Engineers at New Orleans. It is as if Big Red's destiny had come full circle, once again to delight and serve the inhabitants of its environs.

The Founding of Shreveport

Even before men clustered together in cities at the river's edge, the Red River played an important role in their lives. Fishermen farmed watery depths to feed hungry families and earn their meager living. Farmers' children fished on lazy Saturday afternoons, or swam noisily off the river's banks. Churchgoers were baptized in its currents. Families often traveled from place to place in pirogues, rafts, or keelboats. It was only natural that an aggregation of people to whom the river was a necessity should eventually form a city.

With the westward migration from the northern and eastern parts of the United States in the early 1830s, settlers were attracted to Louisiana's fertile lands and agreeable climate, but discouraged by the condition of the river. For the Red had degenerated into little more than one gigantic log jam, with spaces of clear river between the miles of mammoth pile-ups. For years, the gradual and steady accumulation of floating debris within the river had bottlenecked at narrow points, bends, and curves of the river; eventually called "The Great Raft," this log jam obstructed the stream for 160 miles above Natchitoches, rendering the river virtually impassable, even to the Indians.

Facing relocation in an area where the river was virtually useless as a mode of transportation, settlers tended to avoid this area of northern Louisiana, thus retarding its development. It was not until the early 1830s that pioneer river man Captain Henry Miller Shreve was called upon to clear the obstruction.

In 1833, Shreve, along with a considerable company of men and snagboats, began his back-breaking labor at Campti, Louisiana. By 1835, he had navigated as far upstream as the Caddo Indian settlement where Shreveport now stands. Something of a visionary in regards to the river, Shreve saw a strategic site for a one-day important trade center to the fertile tri-state area. It is from this time forward that the exploration and development of northern Louisiana truly began.

The primitive Indian encampment that first caught Shreve's eye was located nine miles south of the present city at the old Peach Blossom bluff on the left bank of Bayou Pierre. In July, 1835, the Caddo Indians signed a treaty transferring all their lands, excepting 640 acres, to the United States. The price of the sale was $80,000.

In a generous gesture that was to prove the genesis of Shreveport, the Indians gave this 640 acres of land to their white interpreter, Larkin Edwards. Edwards later sold his land to the Shreve Town Company for $5,000. Comprised of eight enterprising businessmen—Angus McNeil, Bushrod Jenkins, William Bennett, James Cain, Henry Miller Shreve, Sturgis Sprague, Thomas Taylor Williamson and James Belton Pickett—the Shreve Town Company formed a pact to give the fledgling town an auspicious start. Each man agreed to contribute his portion of the expense to build a "suitable house for public entertainment, steam saw mill, and such other improvements as may be deemed necessary to advance the prosperity of the town." Thus was born a town, carrying within it the seeds of a burgeoning city.

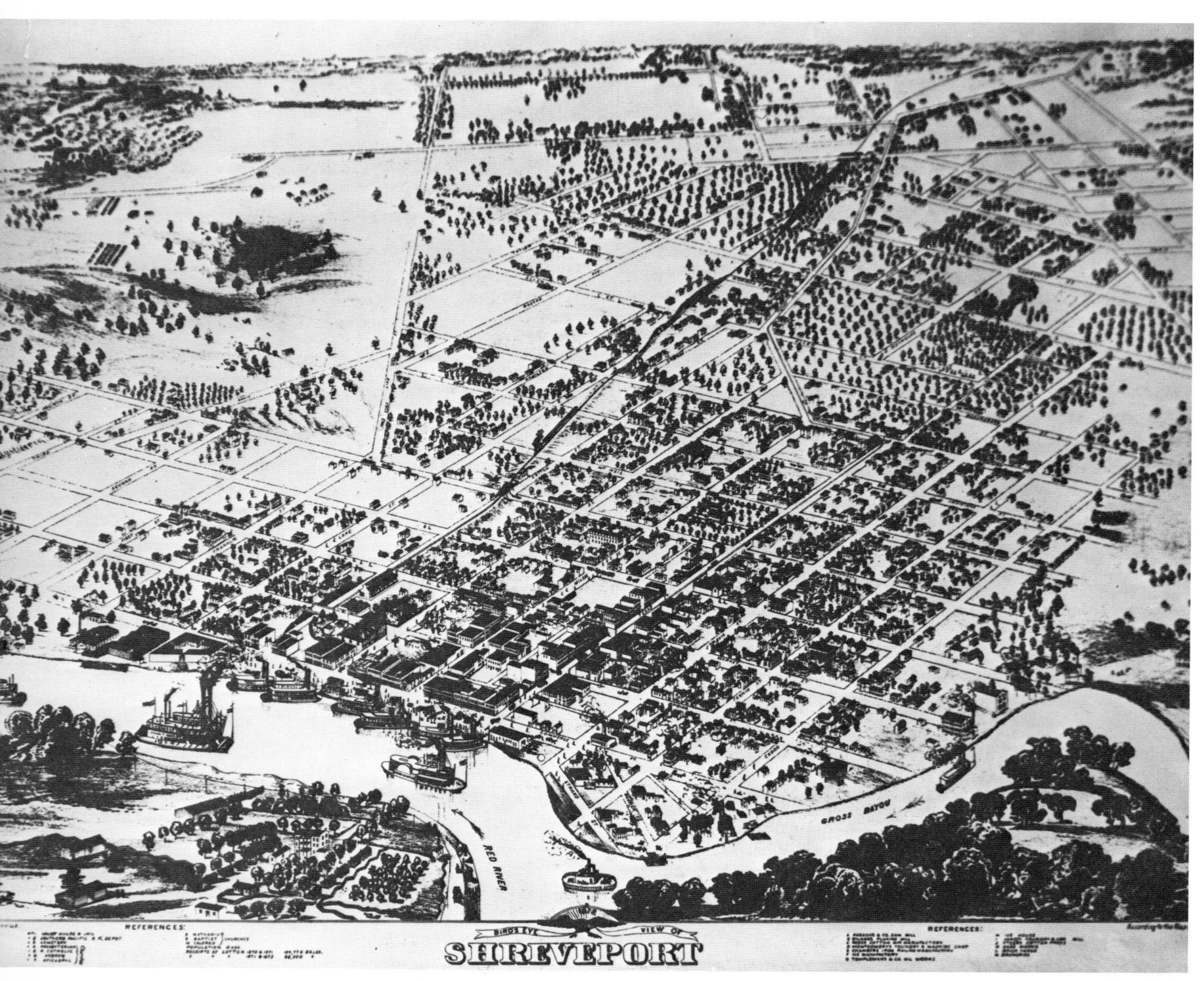

A "bird's eye view" of Shreveport in 1872

The west bank of the river was settled first, with people building homes and farms inland as the country developed. Early Shreveport boasted two main roads, Commerce and Texas streets. Texas Street was considered primarily an access road, with the bulk of activity located directly on the riverfront. "The levee," as Commerce Street was usually called, was the downtown Shreveport of the mid-nineteenth century, with the 500-600 blocks boasting the highest concentration of buildings, due to easy access to transportation and trade. Most of the buildings in this area can be traced back to around 1885, with many tenants of this wholesale district dealing in cotton, groceries and produce. Even today, many of the descendants of the original owners carry on traditional grocery and produce wholesale businesses in the same buildings peopled by their families for almost a century.

Because Texas had recently (1836) gained its independence, four of the first eight streets developed were named for Texas heroes of the Alamo: Fannin, Travis, Texas and Crockett. The other streets, all parallel, were Caddo, Milam, Cotton and Lake. Each of these routes culminated, naturally enough, at the future center of the city's activity, the riverfront. Cross streets were also developed running parallel to the riverfront: Commerce, Spring, Market, Edwards, Marshall, McNeil and Common.

Shreve Town, soon to become Shreveport, became a port of entry into Texas for the western migration. In 1838 the state legislature created Caddo Parish, and in 1839 Shreveport was made the seat of justice for the parish. Five trustees were empowered to collect taxes up to $1,000. John A. Sewall, later killed in a duel along the banks of the Red River, was elected the town's first mayor. And so began the town's affairs.

When Captain Shreve was recalled in 1841, because of the election of the Whigs, Thomas Taylor Williamson, another of the town's founding fathers, agreed to undertake the task of keeping the Red River open for the next five years. Although Shreve had accomplished miracles in clearing mile upon mile of the Great Raft, debris began to accumulate again throughout the ensuing years, creating more log jams and concomitant navigational problems. As the last of the jams was cleared and the Red River finally became a true artery of transportation, Sherevport grew in importance as a river port, both to steamboat owners and later to railroad entrepreneurs. This growing importance embarked the city upon an era of prosperity and growth, particularly after the Civil War.

It is an interesting note in the history of the city that Shreveport served as the Confederate capital of the state of Louisiana during the Civil War, due to its river location. The Red was a natural artery for transporting food, munitions, horses and men from west to south; and during the Civil War period thirty-one different ironclad or tinclad battleships were launched at Shreveport's Levee Docks. Because of the river's vital importance to the Confederacy, Federal troops repeatedly attempted to penetrate its waters and capture Shreveport. Such attempts were often foiled because the Red's low waters prevented the Federal fleet from navigating upriver.

After the Civil War surrender, Shreveport, like countless other towns throughout the Confederacy, was in a turmoil. In addition to widespread looting, public documents were strewn in the streets, with Union troops liberally issuing Confederate stockpiles. Local citizens were made to bow to

Federal will through carpetbaggers, scalawags, and others who dominated Louisiana government at the time, with the Freedmen's Bureau and military rule their strongarm. Southern whites retaliated by forming a white supremacy group, the Knights of the White Camellia; in 1873, however, the White League was established, its purpose to rid government of the carpetbaggers and scalawags and re-establish a benevolent relationship with blacks.

In what must be considered a dark period in Shreveport's history, Caddo and DeSoto parishes finally came to the end of their ropes with Louisiana Reconstruction rule. In 1873, the two parishes unsuccessfully attempted to be annexed to Texas. The horror of Reconstruction finally ended for Shreveport, as it did for the entire South, with the election of U.S. President Rutherford B. Hayes and Louisiana Governor Francis T. Nicholls.

From 1866 to the early 1900s, the city enjoyed a period of mainly prosperity and good fortune, which was nevertheless beset with trials. A nationwide economic depression culminated in the Panic of 1873. That same year, a horrifying yellow fever epidemic swept the entire city, taking the lives of 750 Shreveporters before the swath of destruction it cut through the town was ended.

The work of a religious order from France, the Daughters of the Cross, in 1868 culminated in the construction of one of Shreveport's most famous historic buildings, the old St. Vincent's Motherhouse. These hardy nuns

St. Vincent's Academy

purchased the Captain Leroy M. Nutt plantation at Fairfield Hill, at that time located just outside Shreveport, for $13,000. The original St. Vincent's Academy was part of a complex of stately red brick buildings built by the nuns which later became the United States Motherhouse for the Daughters of the Cross. Destroyed in the 1970s, the historic old buildings made way for a modern shopping mall, appropriately named Mall St. Vincent in memory of its predecessor.

The 1880s saw Shreveport develop as a significant rail center. The construction of the Grand Opera House in 1888 was stimulated by millionaire Jay Gould's visit to the city, seeking the right of way for a north-south rail line to Hope, and thereby shortening the existing route to St. Louis and Chicago. The Opera House was built on the corner of Edwards and Texas streets, and featured such prominent artists as Paderewsky, Sarah Bernhardt, Lillian Russell, John McCormick, and Maurice Chevalier.

Most of the buildings downtown date from the 1870s, a time when Milam Street was almost entirely residential, as it remained into the twentieth century. The muddy street was eventually paved in a rather unique way: Mayor R.N. McKellar began a policy of sentencing city offenders to a fine of $7.50, or 1000 bricks, to be laid first on Texas Street, then on Milam Street!

A typical turn-of-the-century home on Milam Street had a porch level with the sidewalk, with the porch entrance on the side. The courthouse was a "red brick monstrosity with turrets." There was a charming ice cream

The Opera House

shop on Milam, and a perfect Sunday afternoon treat was to have an ice cream and take a ride on the mule-driven streetcar. By 1889, Shreveport also boasted electric, belt-driven streetcars, charging ten cents, the same fare charged by the mule-driven variety. It now seems ironic that Shreveport had electric streetcars in commercial service even before New Orleans!

The future of the city's economic industry revolved around the 1870 discovery of natural gas, incidentally found as a water well was being dug to supply the city's ice factory. The supply was given very little importance at the time, being used only to light the plant. The oil and gas boom of later years, however, was to transform the economy of the area throughout the early and middle part of the twentieth century.

Shreveport's new electric streetcars lined up beside the old Captain Shreve Hotel in the 1890s

The first oil well in this area was drilled in 1904, considered commercially significant only for the kerosene that could be extracted from the oil. In fact, at that time oil producers dumped one of its by-products as waste . . . a by-product known as gasoline! With the coming of aviation and automobiles, the demand for gasoline increased, making the oil industry even more productive and valuable to the economy.

The oil and gas business, along with lucrative lumbering activity, brisk cotton trade and a growing rail system, gave impetus to a growth spurt for Shreveport. From 1900 to 1910, population increased from 16,013 to 28,015.

The city continued to grow in great leaps, adding more cultural and aesthetic institutions as it went. Centenary College, a private Methodist-sponsored liberal arts institution, was chartered in 1825. In 1911, the Saenger Theater was built. And in 1924 W.K. Henderson purchased WCAQ radio and turned it into the still-popular KWKH. Famous for his chatty broadcasting style (featuring no advertising!) and "Hello World" coffee, which sold at a dollar a pound when store-bought coffee was eight cents, Henderson merchandised the tiny radio station into "The Friendly Giant" heard across the United States.

Even though financial depression struck the country in 1929, Shreveport stood firm, shored up by state and federal construction early in the thirties. The downtown municipal airport was completed in 1931, with Barksdale Air Force Base built in 1933 and enlarged in 1939. The State Exhibit Building on the fair grounds was also constructed in 1939.

During World War II, Louisiana bustled with military preparations, while her citizens grappled with nationwide wartime measures such as gasoline, food, and shoe rationing, the conversion of local industries to war needs, and the planting of victory gardens. The escort vessel USS *Shreveport* was christened July 5, 1943, and placed in convoy duty against the Germans and Japanese.

Struggling to provide for a population which had tripled since the 1920s, Shreveport had only five years to recuperate from World War II. Just as the city again turned its attention to the aesthetic side of life with the founding of the Shreveport Symphony, its citizens were called to mobilize for the American "police action" in Korea. This war effort saw many area residents once more pressed into active duty.

The Greater Shreveport Improvement Program was undertaken in 1947, under the guidance of then-Mayor Clyde E. Fant. The $9,600,000 plan was formulated to improve drainage, sewerage, trash and garbage disposal; the water supply; streets; recreation; municipal fire protection; another municipal airport; traffic control; and City Hall.

In 1950 a new city charter reformed government structure which had been in effect since 1910. Barksdale had been designated a Strategic Air Command base in 1949, and the headquarters of the Second Air Force. Shreveport World War II hero, Major William T. "Billy" Whisner, Jr., was given a hero's welcome, having shot down twenty-one Communist jets and damaged seven more.

Throughout the fifties industrial expansion took the forefront, with oil and gas the mainstays of the local economy. It was a decade filled with accomplishments: the renovation of the Youree Hotel, renamed the Captain Shreve in 1952; native Shreveporter Van Cliburn's success in Moscow; the construction of the Marjorie Lyons Playhouse; and the national reputation of the Louisiana Hayride. For the first time the city could turn its full attention to improving the quality of life for *all* of its citizens, increasing school construction and enforcing stricter housing codes for the benefit of the area's black residents.

The 1960s brought both political and economic change. The need for revitalizing the downtown area became evident with the growth and success of suburban shopping centers, and a series of studies was begun in 1965 to suggest ways of breathing new life into downtown. Oil and gas companies, prominent among them United Gas, which had become Pennzoil-United, began to withdraw to other centers of the petroleum industry. Filling the gap, civic leaders attracted new industries: General Electric, Beaird-Poulan, Kast Metals, Gould Battery Plant, Riley-Beaird, Bingham Willamette Company, and Western Electric gave the city an economic shot in the arm with more jobs and capital. In addition, the establishment of Louisiana State University in Shreveport, Southern University in Shreveport, and the LSU Medical School in Shreveport enhanced the academic atmosphere.

A return to the riverfront marked the direction of the 1970s, with widespread renovation throughout the area and new building programs giving a new energy to what was originally the heart of the city. In the 139 years since its incorporation, the town had grown into a medium-sized metropolis, with a population estimated in 1978 at 353,000. The city itself is estimated at more than 208,000. The growth spurt of the fifties has now carried through the sixties and seventies.

The Louisiana State Fair currently draws more than half a million visitors during its annual ten-day run in October, and Holiday in Dixie is a spring classic and the largest parade and beauty-filled spectacular of its kind in the Southwest. The American Rose Society's new $1 million national headquarters and Rose Center are located in Shreveport; it is the home office for the largest plant organization in the United States.

The center of the city is reaching upward, with new high rise buildings altering the skyline. Skyscrapers now reflect in Big Red's muddy waters where once only wagon roads lay. And the river watches its child of a city, spawned from the turbulent waters of its past, grow back toward its origins, toward the place where it all began, the Red River.

Commercial National Bank about 1925

Shreveport firefighters in 1906

Commerce Street about 1920

Nineteenth-century Texas Street

A successful North Louisiana drilling attempt in 1912. By this time, the economic potential of the region's oil and gas was becoming evident.

The stately Shreveport central fire station in 1929

Shreveport City Hall in 1916, serving as information center for the Louisiana State Fair

The Great Raft

The Great Raft was one of those gradual occurrences that one day springs full-blown into public consciousness as a major problem. Year after oblivious year, logs and floating debris caught in bends of the river, bottlenecked where banks narrowed, piled up, one on top of another, until suddenly a vital navigational route was all but impassable.

In spite of the Great Raft, the first steamboat had appeared on the Red in 1814. This signalled the beginning of a new era of navigation on the river, though passage to the rich lands of northwest Louisiana was certainly hindered by the log accumulation, which not only blocked navigation but caused overflows.

The demand for clearing the enormous jam, however, was more immediate. By 1830 the government had set aside a reservation for the Indians in Oklahoma (then called Indian Territory) and had built an army post at Fort Townson. Army supplies sent to the fort had to traverse a series of bypasses around the river that constituted weeks of additional and unnecessary travel time. The conclusion was simple: dismantle the Great Raft, freeing the Red River as the logical navigational route. The solution was rather more difficult, involving an effort that seemed well nigh impossible to even the most optimistic.

Caused partly by caving banks in the upper river which threw trees into the stream, the huge jam stretched from Campti, Louisiana, at its lower end, north to about the Arkansas line, a distance of approximately 160 miles. After each flood, the river's banks gave up more ground to the insatiable waters. Trees, logs and other debris caught on sand bars. The resultant series of jams became water-soaked with time; logs sank to the bottom, and other logs floating down the river became piled up on top of them. When Captain Henry Miller Shreve first encountered the Great Raft, he confronted a log jam twenty-five feet deep, cemented with centuries of packed silt and vegetation roots—solid as rock. Government engineers had reported that any attempt to remove the barrier would "cost a titanic, but futile, effort."

Captain Shreve had cut his teeth on overcoming what to others seemed insurmountable obstacles. Of resolute Quaker heritage, he was brought up on the headwaters of the Ohio and early on became enfevered with a love of rivers. He began flatboating as a young man, and it was due to his eventual efforts toward improved steamboat efficiency and safety testing equipment that landmark safety legislation was brought about.

In 1824, Shreve, already a well-known inventor and engineer, devised a steam snagboat, which he utilized in clearing snags and other obstructions from the Mississippi River earlier in his career. Something of a legendary river man for this reason, he then offered the federal government a plan to rid the Red River of its obstruction. Thus, in 1833, about to retire at the age of 48, he suddenly found himself back "up to his snagboat" in the log jam clearing business.

Shreve's steamboat ram was a precursor of the deadly rams used later on western waters during the Civil War. When the *Archimedes* steamed into sight at Campti one early April morning in 1833, a more awkward and ungainly sight could not be imagined. Looking like two steamboats joined near the waterline with heavy timbers, there was a broad alleyway left between the hulls. Above this alleyway between the twin hulls was a steam

Captain Shreve directs the assault on the great raft.
Painting © 1970 by the R.W. Norton Art Gallery, Shreveport, La.

Even after being cleared, the raft was continually reforming. This scene was during the 1870s.

windlass, the shaft of which weighed more than seven thousand pounds. This windlass provided the power for the *Archimedes* to deal with even the largest, most stubborn logs.

Alongside the *Archimedes* appeared three smaller steamboats: *Souvenir*, *Java*, and *Pearl*. Shreve's total crew was comprised of 159 men, including officers, mechanics, laborers and cooks. At daylight on April 11, 1833, they set to work dismantling one of the most unyielding log jams ever encountered.

The work was exhausting, but the initial results were encouraging, as the first year's efforts concentrated mainly on already-decaying portions of the raft. Men on rafts and in skiffs worried heavy cables through the snags and willows to the large timber in the raft. They went first after the biggest trees, using the windlass to dislodge them. Engineers poured out cable from the machine, the windlass wound up, and trees came crashing to the alleyway between the hulls, to be sawed into more manageable lengths and tumbled off at the rear.

Tearing out the larger trees allowed dirt and rotted drift to wash away, exposing "choctaws"—ancient, preserved logs—which could then be uprooted and sawed into smaller pieces. Small steamers, skiffs, and rafts drove all the floating logs and chunks into a bayou, where they were rammed tight by running a steamboat into them time after time. This effort dammed the bayous, forcing the Red to flow faster in its own banks and cut silt from the bottom to make a good channel.

The effort of clearing such a massive log jam was tremendous. Days were hot. Eyes watered and noses ran in the mosquito smudges. In fact, insects were one of the men's greatest problems, as they smeared themselves with mud to discourage flies, wasps, and hornets. Snakes were everywhere. And soon crew members began to fall sick, four men dying of cholera. Limited in money, Captain Shreve was continually called away from his work on the Great Raft to work on other rivers.

As more solid portions of the raft were reached, the work slowed. Seventy-one miles of the log jam were removed in the first year, 1833, but by 1837, only 12 ¾ miles had been removed during the entire fourth year of work. Government snag boats were employed to keep new jams from forming, widening the river by pulling out or sawing off the logs imbedded in the river banks.

U.S. Army snagboat Aid *at work around 1873*

Snagboat work was hazardous as well as back-breaking.

Finally, on March 7, 1838, Shreve reached the head of the raft, between Cowhide Bayou and Cedar Bluffs. He had accomplished his task, eliminating the massive log jam at a total cost of $300,000, less than ten percent of its previous estimates. But the saga of the Great Raft did not end there. Recalled in 1841 because of the election of the Whigs to office, Shreve was not able to complete his job of keeping the Red clear of log jams. Despite his initial success, federal funds were not appropriated to keep the raft from reforming, and private efforts to keep the river clear of snags and log jams were terminated by the Civil War.

By July, 1838, a new raft 2,300 feet long had formed three miles below the head of the old raft. Captain Thomas Taylor Williamson, a co-founder of Shreve Town with Shreve himself, undertook the task of keeping the river open for the next five years. In 1843, another raft formed at Carolina Bluffs, below the raft opened by Shreve in 1838. This obstruction was not completely removed until 1872-73, this time by Lieutenant E.A. Woodruff, U.S. Army.

It was many years later before the upper river was finally cleared of its jams. Steamboats going upstream before that time went through 12 Mile Bayou and Soda Lake, and from there on to Jefferson, Texas. When the upper river was finally cleared in 1873, the steamboats were able to take a more direct route, bypassing Jefferson. Indeed, even the railroad eventually went around Jefferson, sealing the doom of the once-bustling metropolis.

While steamboat service through to Shreveport probably did not fully blossom until the late 1830s, navigation on the Red River was one of the most salient factors in the development of the city as a thriving commercial center. The River thus ultimately became navigable from its mouth north for a distance of about 720 miles. The entire upper Red River Valley was finally open to cultivation and settlement.

Henry Miller Shreve died in St. Louis in 1851. During his lifetime, he had done more than any other person toward swift, safe passage of the Mississippi and its tributaries. He had pioneered in the invention and development of the steam snagboat, and pushed for innovative safety legislation for steamboat travel. It is said that his removal of the Great Raft did more than any other single act of any one person to affect the lives of people in northwestern Louisiana.

The Steamboat Era

That rich period of time which conjures up images of Tara, Mark Twain and graceful Southern belles twirling lacy parasols must of necessity include the nostalgic and evocative figure of the steamboat. The century-old cry, "Steamboat 'round the bend!" held more than the promise of mere transportation; it was a call to social life, beckoning all within walking or riding distance to celebrate its arrival.

Red River heard the whistle of its first steamboat in December, 1814—before the river was entirely open to navigation. The boat was Captain Henry Miller Shreve's *Enterprise*, which he plied up the Red to contest the rights of Fulton to navigate western waters by steam propelled boats. During the steamboats' heyday, in the 1850s and early 1860s particularly, 844 boats made regular stops at 542 different landings, from Jefferson, Texas, to the Mississippi River. All but a comparative few of these boats were freight haulers, with cargo varying from cotton and produce to cattle. Steamboats continued to navigate the Red, of course, after the interruption of the Civil War, but somehow steamboating never reached the heights it had attained in pre-war days.

Even the names of the old Red River steamboats are enough to evoke the sights and sounds of a bygone era. Boats were often named after real people, but more often than not their names reflected the romantic feeling of the time. Names like *Flirt*, *Flora*, *Frolic*, *Echo*, *Any One*, *Dawn*, *Effort*, *Flint*, *Home*, *Hornet*, *Hustler*, *Independence*, *Live Oak*, *Lotus*, *Mars*, *Meteor*, *Messenger*, *Music*, *Newsboy*, *Planter*, *Right Way*, *Seven Up*, *Starlight*, *Storm*, *Telegraph*, *Swamp Fox*, *Venture*, *Victory*, *Whisper*, and *White Cloud* were typical of the fleets.

There were two *Shreveports*, two *Belles of Shreveport,* three *Louisianas*, four *Caddos*, six *Texases*, four *Teches*, three *Alexandrias*, two *Bossiers*, two *Arkansas,* four *Swamp Foxes*, *Monroes*, *Cotton Valleys*, *Bastrops* and *DeSotos*.

The Columbia *ties up at a Red River wharf during high water.*

The Red River Line, founded in 1881, boasted "first class steamers John D. Scully, Marie Louise, Kate Kinney, Danube, Yazoo Valley, Jessie K. Bell, Silver City, W.J. Behan, Alexandria, Cornie Brandon, J.G. Fletcher, Jewel, and Frank Willard," in an old advertisement taken from the Shreveport City Directory. The ad expounded further: "Close connection at Shreveport with Texas and Pacific Railway Co. to all points in northern and western Texas, and at New Orleans with Morgan's Line of Steam Ships to all points north and east."

Steamboat landings were no less prosaically named: Look Out, One Eye, Once More, Virgin's Camp, Echo, Hard Times, Blue Lights, I.O.U., You Bet, Devil's Elbow, Last Chance, Da Da, Opossum Trot, High Die, Telegram, Lovely Point, White House, Omega, Home Place, Glover's Bar and Boytown.

Among the leading operators on the river in the busiest times were the Red River Packet Company, with daily departures of boats from Shreveport to New Orleans; the Carter Lines, with boats running between Shreveport and St. Louis; the Red River and Coast Line, with eighteen boats on the upper and lower Red River; and the G.L. Kouns and Bros. Line, the largest of all the ownerships. The Kouns line ran a boat up Red River which was a pioneer of their line of boats, called the *Era*, numbering from one to thirteen—for as one boat wore out, another new one numerically took its place. Smaller boats generally ran from Shreveport up, larger ones from Shreveport down.

The *Era No. 5*, with Captain Noah Scovell in command, was captured by the Federal gunboat *Queen of the West* near Alexandria during the

Civil War. The captain was made prisoner, and all the black deck crew and freight were seized by the gunboat and carried up the Mississippi River to St. Louis. How the captain disposed of the boat was never known. The black crew was put off on an island, and it was many days before they were rescued and returned to their owners.

Around 1850 larger and more luxurious passenger boats began to appear, some 200 and 300 feet in length, with individual cabins, dining and entertainment halls. The showboats even featured stages: the *Banjo* had a stage at the end of one deck, and at one time performed a minstrel show for the Gaiety Theatre of Shreveport in September, 1860. *Era No. 11* was even large enough to warrant publishing its own daily newspaper on board in 1870. The *Jessie K. Bell*, a famous deluxe sidewheeler, made the journey to Shreveport once a year, to take the ''northerners'' down to Mardi Gras.

Of the more luxurious steamboats, few could rival the *R.H. Powell* in elegance. A typical menu:

> March 27, 1855. Soup: green turtle. Fish: Baked, red, plain sauce, broiled sheepshead, oyster sauce; broiled chicken, leg Creole mutton, caper sauce, turkey, fresh beef tongue, ham, corned beef, pork and beans; Entrees: gelatin poulard, allspice jelly, magalenes of whiting a la Venetienne; patted chaud of godveiau a la ciboulette; breast of mutton, braised with green peas; gelatin turkey, with allspice jelly; stuffed shoulder of mutton, garnished with oysters; tenderloin steak with French fried potatoes; gelatin hogshead, allspice jelly; hogshead a la Florentine; stuffed crabs and oyster pie, roast beef, mutton, veal, pork, pig; Vegetables: Irish potatoes, boiled, mashed, creamed, turnips, sweet potatoes, celery, hominy, cabbage, radishes, parsnips, lettuce; Game: wild turkey, maitre d'hote sauce; saddle of venison, cranberry sauce, guava jelly; Dessert: currant, apple, cranberry and cherry pie; pound, jelly, sponge and fruit cakes; tartlets, french puffs, currant puddings, orange, Madeira and transparent jellies; vanilla and lemon custards, ice cream, cream cakes; Fruits: pineapples, oranges, bananas, apples, figs, raisins, prunes, almonds, pecans English walnuts, filberts, Brazil and cream nuts; Wines: claret, white wines and Java coffee.

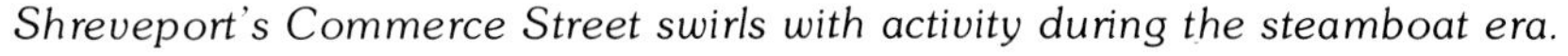

Shreveport's Commerce Street swirls with activity during the steamboat era.

Millions of North Louisiana cotton bales went to market on the riverboats.

Captain Shreve began the custom of having the names of different states painted on the cabin doors of his steamers. Thus, passengers from Oklahoma could have the cabin named "Oklahoma," and so on. The origin of the word "staterooms" comes from this unique practice.

Building a steamboat at the wharf was a civic project, shared by all in the community. The completion and launching of a boat became the occasion for a public celebration. In fact, dances and parties were often held at any city where the steamboats docked long enough. Since every commodity, necessity and luxury of life came by river steamboat, it is only natural that the city's life, both commercial and social, centered around the river.

The average steamboat at that time was a combination post office, general store, bank, brokerage office, sales market, prison, and medical center all in one. Some boats were specialized, as in the case of *Col. T.G. Sparks*, a prison penitentiary boat. The cabin deck of the *Sparks* was enclosed with iron bars, and all the crew, except for the officers, was comprised of convicts. The *City Belle* was transformed into a Civil War hospital for Federal troops in 1864, carrying eighteen hundred sick and wounded men from devastated Vicksburg, Mississippi.

Steamboat travel under the best of circumstances could be quite hazardous. The boats were wooden, often carrying inflammable cargo, and with the added presence of boilers and machinery to get up steam, there was the constant danger of fire and explosions. In addition, the Red River was narrower than it is today, and waters in connecting swamps, lakes, and bayous kept it at a more constant level.

The B. T. Bryarly *moves gingerly through a narrow, snag-filled stretch of the Red.*

Trees overhanging the water, hidden snags, sandbars and other obstacles sank boats continually . . . in fact, the Red River soon became known as the "steamboat graveyard." In 1886, the *Lizzie Hamilton* included watermelons in her cargo to use under her bow when she became hung on sandbars during low water. Many of the lighter craft of the old river were eighteen inches and even eleven inches draught.

During the mid-1800s, one of the hazards of the river was the falls at Alexandria. These falls caused great trouble, delay and expense to boats that plied Red River. During the low water months of summer, passengers and freight often transferred to lighter boats to continue to Shreveport. The falls were, after several previous efforts, finally blasted out permanently.

Passengers seeking cheap passage slept on the main deck, along with the boilers, machinery, and cord wood kept for fuel, in addition to any freight the ship might be carrying. Passengers at this level furnished their own meals and bedding, fending off mosquitoes, humid, sultry weather, and occasionally sickness as well.

One pictures the steamboat as a leisurely, lazy sort of water vehicle, gracefully floating its way down the placid river, lost in its own time. Such was not the case, however. In 1837, the *Marmora* ran into the *Black Hawk* near Shreveport, occasioning the first lawsuit ever brought for damages in river navigation. The charge: careless and reckless steering. Boats often raced with each other, creating a traffic hazard. In 1866, all previous speed records were broken when the *Anne Everson,* a sidewheeler, steamed from Alexandria to Shreveport in fifty-two hours.

Rates for passage and freight varied, dependent upon the water conditions. High water brought low rates, low water high rates. In addition, the harvest season brought higher rates on farm produce. In July of 1854, the *Augusta,* traveling between Jefferson, Texas, and New Orleans in high water times, charged $1 per bale of cotton, or per bull. During low water it charged up to $10 for bulls, $10 to $25 for bales of cotton, and $7 per barrel. The *St. Charles* collected $15 per passenger from Shreveport to New Orleans during high water, with the price skyrocketing to $40 per passenger during low water. One particular boat of the G.L. Kouns line once cleared $20,000 on one trip from New Orleans to Shreveport. The profit from the journey was used to build a new boat.

During the height of the riverboat traffic, a daily newspaper column was published called "River Intelligence." This column carried news of weather, river conditions, and steamboat occurrences, many of which were quite humorous. Because of the importance of the steamboat to the life of the city, "River Intelligence" was often the most widely-read part of the newspaper.

Steamboats were also used as ferries between Shreveport and Bossier until the early Vicksburg, Shreveport and Pacific Railroad bridge was built. Many wrecks were associated with this ferry service. In 1873, Shreveport was hit with a yellow fever epidemic that nearly wiped out the city. It was widely believed that the stench of cattle drowned when a steamboat sank in the outlying harbor was the cause of the epidemic.

The beginning of the end for the steamboat trade came in 1858, when the first railroad was built. The Southern Pacific constructed its line from the western boundary of Louisiana, at Swanson's Landing on Caddo Lake, to El Paso, Texas. Ironically enough, steamboats were essential in ferrying supplies for the railway construction up and down the Red. When the Civil War temporarily halted the building of the railroads, steamboats gained a new importance. The boats normally plying passengers and freight on the river now distributed the produce of Texas and Louisiana to the Mississippi River, from there to be transported to the war-torn Eastern states.

The Great Raft was finally cleared, for the last time, in 1873—but it was too late for the steamboat. By then the railroads had gained enough of a foothold to be permanently entrenched, and the doughty old boats never quite reclaimed their lost trade. The completion of the Vicksburg, Shreveport and Pacific railway line in 1885 and of the Texas and Pacific line to New Orleans sealed the doom of the river trade. The graceful steamboat became a nostalgic remnant of a bygone era, relegated to a place in the annals of history.

Civil War

The Red River Campaign

Ever since the days of the earliest explorers, the Red River has bristled with military significance. The French and Spanish sent military expeditions along its wayward course; forts and presidioes clustered near its banks. When the Spanish claimed territory in Texas, several expeditions used the Red to invade that state: notably Augustus William Magee and Bernardo Guterrez De Lara who rendezvoused at Natchitoches; and James Long, whose force gathered at Natchez in 1819.

But at no time was the Red River more important to the entire South than during the Civil War. It was a natural center for military operations, and it might be easily said that no other river save the Mississippi was so vital to the Confederacy.

Immediately after the outbreak of the war, the Confederate government required the registration of all river boats at the old United States Custom House in New Orleans. As the conflict reached its second year, the Red gained in importance to the Confederacy, and Shreveport and Jefferson, Texas, both key ports, fairly bustled with river activity. Troops were recruited and steamed away to the east on Red River boats.

During the beginning years, crucial battles were fought almost solely in the eastern part of the Confederacy, with western peoples furnishing supplies. As a blockade by the Union Navy made the shipment of goods to the east by sea impossible, thoughts naturally turned to the Red River as the next choice of routes. Many articles of war began to enter the eastern states by way of Mexico, Texas and the river.

In order to safeguard the war supplies on their way downriver, the Confederates strengthened their troops at Port Hudson, near the mouth of the river. On July 8, 1863, Admiral David Farragut and a fleet of Union gunboats stormed Port Hudson from New Orleans, captured the garrison there, and proceeded to blockade the Mississippi River at that point, effectively cutting off the Red River and all of its tributaries with the exception of the LaFourche.

This single event, the cutting off of the Red River route to the east, had a ruinous effect on the eventual outcome of the war. Along with the fall of Vicksburg, the blockade itself was devastating enough to almost guarantee the loss of the entire war for the Confederacy. The resulting starvation and want merely hastened the end.

In 1863 a Navy yard was established at Shreveport, then serving as capital of Louisiana, and a military vessel modeled after the legendary *Merrimac* was planned. The *Missouri* was the only man-of-war ever built on the Red River. Constructed of wood, its slanted sides were covered with iron rails from the Southern Pacific Railroad for protection. The only portion of the ship not entirely covered with iron was the pilot house and wheel, located in the middle of the boat. Ironically enough, the *Missouri* was never given a chance to prove its potential; it was eventually surrendered without having fired a single shot.

The Union ironclad Essex *on the Mississippi prior to the Red River campaign.*

The state of Texas seemed a particularly desirable foothold to the Federal armies at that time. The army of Napoleon III was making progress in nearby Mexico, with whisperings that the French had an eye cocked toward Texas itself. For these reasons, President Abraham Lincoln was particularly anxious that the U.S. flag be planted somewhere in Texas, bolstering the Union's position there. In addition, the liberation of the German-American anti-slave citizens of Texas would have been an added source of strength to the Union. Last but certainly not least, rumors of immense cotton holdings in Texas prompted Federal armies to consider an invasion upriver to that state.

Federal General Henry Halleck urged a combined military-naval movement up the Red via Shreveport and thence to the military occupancy of north Texas. This maneuver would not only undermine the French influence, but would separate even more the already divided sections of the Confederacy, and cut off the flow of supplies from Texas to Louisiana and Arkansas. General Nathaniel Banks was put in command of the infantry divisions, while Admiral David Porter pledged the cooperation of the Mississippi River's naval forces. The infamous Red River Campaign had begun.

On March 7, 1864, Porter assembled a massive flotilla comprised of some of the finest vessels in the west. Thirteen ironclads included the *Essex*, *Benton*, *Lafayette*, *Choctaw*, *Chillicothe*, *Ozark*, *Louisville*, *Carondelet*, *Eastport*, *Pittsburgh*, *Mound City*, *Osage*, and *Neosho*. These deeper-draft vessels could provide the necessary armory against riverbank fortifications and heavy ordnance. The seven shallow-draft tinclads, including *Cricket*, *Gazelle*, *Signal*, *Juliet*, *Covington*, *Ouachita* and *FortHindman*, were not as heavily armored for protection, but ideal for navigation up the shallow Red.

The *Lexington* was a timberclad sternwheeler with a background of three years' experience already on the river. Porter's flagship, the *Black Hawk*, gave the orders for the entire fleet, which was rounded out by twenty transports (later increased to thirty). Before the campaign was over, not less than fifteen additional ironclads and gunboats were sent up the Red River as reinforcements—all in all, a formidable force indeed!

On 12 March, the impressive fleet began its move upriver, anticipating a total rout of the poorly-defended Confederates. Opposing the Union naval forces with fewer than a half-dozen vessels, the rebels did seem an easy target. But for once, the unpredictable Red indirectly sprang to the defense of its native sons.

For the first time in years, the river had not risen in the spring as it usually did. As a result, the Federal fleet was severely handicapped, particularly with the deeper-draft ironclads, as it attempted to navigate upriver. At Alexandria, the vessels approached two sets of extremely shallow falls. The rapids were about one mile apart, with only a twenty-foot wide channel between them. The heaviest ironclad, the *Eastport*, was used as a test vessel; it stuck on the rocks, of course, until a slight rise in the water several days later pushed it over the falls. Others eventually followed, along with thirty Army transports.

In the meanwhile, Banks had amassed a large assemblage of troops to negotiate the land route. Ordered to take seventeen thousand men to Alexandria, he was at that point to be joined by ten thousand of General William Tecumseh Sherman's men, "loaned" specifically for the Red River Campaign. General Frederick Steele's fifteen thousand men were to comprise the third part of the infantry, although they never actually arrived. Porter's naval squadron was the final component.

Awaiting their advance was a Confederate force of thirty thousand, headed by General Kirby Smith. But dissension and rivalry had begun to split the Union infantry and naval forces even before their engagement with Smith. For two years, the Mississippi Valley had been a hotbed of cotton speculation, with Union Army and Navy units, as well as civilians, trading illegally with the Confederates and seizing all the cotton they could get their hands on as well. When they arrived in Alexandria, tension between Federal military and naval forces reached its height, mostly over cotton confiscation. Banks was jealous of Porter's early arrival, and subsequent "head start" in seizing the cotton there as a war prize. It would later be contended by the Joint Committee on the Conduct of the War that this preoccupation with cotton and resultant differences between Union troops may have led to the military disaster that followed.

As the Federal army and navy finally began to advance from Alexandria, the Confederates retreated, obstructing the river as much as possible as they went. Sharpshooters, firing from the cover of the thickly forested banks, picked off Union sailors as they attempted to remove the obstructions.

So far, the Union had the advantage in hand: neither army nor navy forces had sustained heavy losses, and Porter's fleet was making slow but certain progress upriver. Then came the turning point of the Red River Campaign: Banks, having followed the river's course closely so far, veered away from it at Grand Ecore, Louisiana, and thus out of protection of the fleet's firepower and its supplies. Surely he must not have known about the road just east of the river that remained close to its bank. For had he chosen this route, it is very likely that, with the added might of Porter's vessels, they might have continued through to the capture and occupation of Shreveport.

Instead, taking an inland road, Banks engaged in hand to hand combat with the Confederate armies, sustaining heavy losses in battle on April 8 and 9. With his forces severely crippled by the blow, Banks was forced to abandon his campaign against Shreveport, and turn back toward Alexandria.

Unseasonably low water in the Spring of 1864 made the river itself a most effective barrier against the Union's Red River campaign.

Meanwhile, Porter's flotilla had reached a point just thirty miles below Shreveport, when they encountered an unusually clever obstruction. The *New Falls City*, a huge steamboat, had been deliberately sunk across the river, with fifteen feet sticking out on the banks on either side. The boat was broken down in the middle, where a sand bar had begun to form over it. Prominently attached to the boat was a formal invitation to the Federals, left by the Confederates, to attend a ball in Shreveport! The obstacle of the boat, combined with unseasonably low water, prompted Porter to exclaim, "That's the smartest thing I've ever known a rebel to do!"

As Porter's men attempted to remove the ship, news came of Banks' sudden and disastrous defeat, and of his retreat toward Alexandria. So close to their goal and yet so far, with orders to turn back, Porter was afraid his own retreat would be interrupted by the enemy's land forces—and he was right. With the way cleared of Banks' troops, Confederate soldiers were free to roam the river's levees, keeping up a fire of musketry at the Union fleet. As he steamed toward Alexandria, Porter ran a gauntlet of both natural and man-made hazards that threatened his return.

Many of his ships ran aground in the shallow waters, and the Confederates increased in numbers as his fleet proceeded downriver at a rate of thirty miles per day. Continuing to harass the boats' passage, rebel infantrymen were nevertheless handicapped by their lack of heavy artillery along the river banks. The curious fight that continued between infantry and gunboats resulted in the destruction of or damage to a great number of Union vessels. The *City Bell*, navigating her way upriver with an Ohio regiment of reinforcements, was even captured by the Confederate army.

Although General Kirby Smith had originally commanded 21,000 troops, only a portion of these could be spared for the protection of the city of Shreveport. Some of the men were positioned along the Gulf Coast to prevent invasion, with additional troops protecting the Mexican border. This left a force of only 16,000 men to repel the Federal attack.

As part of a chain of defense around the area, four forts were built on the city's highest point, three in Shreveport and one across the river in Bossier, then known as Cane City. Sorely pressed for able-bodied men, Smith enlisted the aid of hundreds of slaves in building a line of entrenchments around the city's batteries and forts. At Fort Turnbull, a garrison built nearest the river, the scarcity of heavy armory was critical. Quick thinking and resourcefulness, however, provided a clever solution. In a cunning show of apparent force, the Confederates mounted logs on the river banks to simulate cannon and deceive the enemy as to the fort's real strength. When General John B. Magruder inspected the fort, he exclaimed, "Your forts are only a humbug!" Therefore, Fort Turnbull became Fort Humbug, the name it has been called by area residents since that time.

As both the Union army and navy retreated, they cut a swath of destruction throughout the countryside, looting and burning farms and plantations. The town of Natchitoches sustained heavy damages by fire. And the river continued to fall.

When the fleet reached Alexandria, the falls were too shallow for any of the boats to pass. With the navy's finest engineers at their wits' end, a Lt. Colonel Bailey proposed a unique solution that was at first met with derision. His proposal involved building a 600-foot dam out of trees across the river at the lower falls, thus causing the water to rise and allowing the boats

Fort Humbug today, still bristling with wooden "firepower"

to pass safely. No one thought it would work, but no one had a better suggestion, either. When Bailey's dam was finally in place and the initial rush of water pushed several stalled boats safely over the falls, all present paid tribute to his initially-overlooked engineering genius.

By mid-May, Porter's retreat was complete: he had returned to the mouth of the Red River, and an expedition in which no fewer than seventy vessels took part had come to an ignominious end. Charges and counter-charges were exchanged between Banks and Porter as to who really lost the campaign, but the fact remained that no other important campaign took place along the Red River after this defeat.

Called the "Red River Disaster" by the Joint Committee on the Conduct of the War, the effort was indeed a costly failure for the Federal forces. Banks had suffered the loss of fifty-two hundred men, twenty-one pieces of artillery, over three hundred wagons, and large amounts of supplies. Many boats and naval personnel were also lost. The Confederates lost four thousand men, and some artillery, but little else.

The most serious result of the expedition's failure was the effect it had east of the Mississippi: General A.J. Smith's Federal troops, also involved in the Red River Campaign, did not link up with Sherman's men as expected before his march into Georgia. And Union General Edward Canby's projected campaign against Mobile had to be postponed for ten months because of the disaster. There is no question that the failure of the Red River Campaign lengthened the Civil War.

Bailey's dam under construction

Part of the crew of the Union ironclad Choctaw

The last effort of the Confederate Navy on western waters was a brilliant attempt by Commander C.W. Read to run the Mississippi River blockade with his ram *Webb.* Heavily laden with a load of cotton bound for Havana, Read made a desperate dash through the fleet at the mouth of the Red River, escaping without injury. News of the *Webb*'s escape was telegraphed to New Orleans, but under the guise of an Army transport, she almost passed the waiting Union vessels undetected. When she was recognized, it was too late to stop her. Almost home free, the *Webb* met the steamer *Richmond* twenty miles below New Orleans, who refused to let her through. Rather than allow the Union navy to utilize his ship, Read ran the *Webb* aground and burned her, the crew escaping into the forest on shore.

On June 3, 1865, Lt. Commander W.E. Fitzhugh officially received the surrender of Lt. J.H. Carter and the Confederate naval forces at his command. Four years of military operations along the Red River thus came to an end, with the Red River Campaign long remembered as one of the most resounding and embarrassing Union defeats of the Civil War.

The Coming of the Railroads

In July, 1857, a time of unrivaled prosperity for Red River steamboats, the steamer *Alida* plied her way upriver through the bayou to Caddo Lake and on to Swanson's Landing, Texas. Connected tautly behind her was a barge sporting one of the strangest sights people in the area had yet seen: a railway locomotive. The first one to reach this neck of the woods, the locomotive seemed merely a marvel of new technology, when in fact it was to prove a harbinger of doom for the very steamboat that pulled it toward its destination. For the coming of the railroads was the downfall of the steamboats, and the ultimate cause of the river trade's demise. Temporarily, however, this locomotive had come to serve the river, not to destroy it.

The steamboat interests of the day viewed the coming of the railroads with great favor. They assumed that rail and river interests would work hand in hand, with rail lines serving as "feeders" into the interior and bringing more freight from greater distances to be carried by boats. That there might be a time when these "feeder" roads would all connect, forming a continuous artery of transportation independent of the river, never occurred to the river men. After all, Louisiana's towns and settlements all faced the river—the richest plantations were along its banks. Shreveport's finest businesses were built by the levee. They would always need the river!

From 1816 through 1840, the steamboat reigned as queen over the trade of the river valleys. 1840 to 1860 was a period of prosperity, indeed, but railroads were beginning to appear with increasing mileage. The competition, if not keenly felt, was nevertheless there. And while the interruption of the Civil War almost totally suspended river traffic, most railroad construction was continued in order to supply the armies.

After the war, the steamboat engaged in a fierce but losing battle with the railroads. Never quite able to regain their former places of prominence, the big river ships began to see their freight trade diminishing, their rates undercut by the rail lines and their profits sinking fast. This was especially true along the Red River.

New Orleans had always controlled the trade of the entire Red River Valley, dispatching steamships to churn up and down both the Mississippi and the Red and their tributaries with passengers and freight. In the 1880s, however, much of the cotton that formerly went to New Orleans by the Red River began to go to St. Louis by rail. In 1886, 226,496 bales went by rail from Arkansas to St. Louis, 211,046 bales from Texas, and 2,805 bales from the Indian Territory (Oklahoma). New Orleans' monopoly on trade seemed ready to topple, with St. Louis looming as her most formidable rival.

Construction of the St. Louis, Iron Mountain and Southern Railroad began the rivalry; the Missouri, Kansas and Texas Railroad helped nurture the competition. These rail lines invaded Arkansas, western and northern Louisiana and Texas, all formerly dominated by New Orleans steamship service.

At the time of the encroachment by the railway lines, it was typical of a railroad company to seek its charter under a name indicating its proposed route. It was also fairly common for a company, anxious to interest investors and attract prospective clients, to exaggerate slightly its estimated reach. Thus we find railroads with names that ultimately proved longer than their routes!

Chartered in 1852, the Vicksburg, Shreveport and Texas Railroad began its construction at Delta Point, opposite Vicksburg, and built west, toward Monroe. Work proceeded apace on this portion of the construction, but a planned Shreveport-to-Waskom leg seemed jinxed. By 1861, three separate contractors had tackled the Shreveport-Waskom portion of the railway, with the route still incomplete.

The Texas Western Railroad, also chartered in 1852, was re-organized after the Civil War as the Southern Pacific, a name that would run through Louisiana history well into the twentieth century. While the long-range plans were to build a line from Marshall, Texas, all the way across the state to El Paso, revenue was needed immediately to begin such an ambitious undertaking. A Shreveport-to-Marshall link was suggested, as surveys indicated the profitability of such a line would be high.

An ad in the Shreveport newspaper, May 1866, read as follows: "Wanted, immediately, 500 laborers to work on Southern Pacific railroad. Messrs. Taylor and Abney have contracted to furnish 20,000 cross ties and are in want of more hands to whom they will pay liberal wages. The camp is five miles from town. Transportation free. Best rations served. Desire teams and wagons, also."

By 1868 the Shreveport-Marshall leg was completed. A passenger train left Shreveport daily except Sundays at 1:30 P.M. for Marshall and intermediate stations, and it arrived at Marshall at 5 P.M. The return trip left Marshall at 7 A.M., arriving in Shreveport at 10:30 A.M. Passengers wishing to connect with the stage line at Marshall could travel to many other points from there; those towns not covered by the stage could be reached by renting horses and vehicles from two large livery stables.

The long-range plans of the Southern Pacific, however, were never realized. In 1871, the tottering railroad was taken over by the Texas and

Pacific, a railway line with far more ambitious plans: to build a line all the way to the Pacific Ocean! Its plans proceeded rather more quickly, with the line reaching Dallas in 1873, El Paso in 1881, and finally California in 1890.

The construction of the Texas and Pacific was perhaps the severest blow dealt the river. It was the first railroad in the region to run parallel to the Red River, and thus was in competition with it at many points. The railroad's route ran along the Mississippi River to Baton Rouge, cutting thence in a northwesterly direction, crossing the Atchafalaya River, and running parallel to the Red all the way to Sherman, Texas. By 1887 the Texas and Pacific claimed to take 40 percent of all the trade at points where it came into competition with the river route.

A Texas and Pacific station in 1918

RIVER-RAIL COMPETITION		
Year	Bales	
	Shipped by River	Shipped by Rail
1877-78	193,800	—
78-79	145,119	—
79-80	144,616	—
80-81	186,585	—
83-84	104,039	140,198
84-85	54,726	197,632
85-86	61,661	223,898
86-87	55,128	322,538

These figures show a sudden and decided decrease in river traffic after the coming of the railroad. The river men made appeals to the public, reduced their rates, and tried to run the boats on a more economical basis, but never quite regained their lost trade. Railroads cut their rates at all competing points on the river, making up the difference at the non-competing points by advancing freight rates, sometimes as much as 25 to 100 percent. The steamboats, of course, were rendered helpless; since most boats were independently operated, an increase in rates would mean they had to compete with each other, as well as the railroad lines. Adding to their problems was the fact that the time when business was best, the fall, was also the time when water was lowest, and navigation at its most difficult.

The Houston and Texas Central, constructed in 1873, with its northern terminus the town of Denison, Texas, worsened matters. The trade of the area, formerly utilizing the Red River, was deflected southward to Houston and Galveston. To add insult to injury, the Santa Fe Railway, with its route from Kansas City to Galveston, also cut through the Red River area west of Houston and Texas Central, further severing the river from the trade areas it had formerly been dependent upon.

Colonel Mason, a reporter for the Shreveport *Times* "River and Weather" column, chronicled the activity surrounding the boats on the levee. He described the riverfront of this period, 1873, with plenty of boats in port but nothing to do:

> Yesterday was one of the dullest days we have experienced on the landing. From early morning till dewy eve there was not the first thing doing. Not a steamer was expected from any source upon which to base even a hope of something stirring. The Belle Rowland and the Clifford had the landing proper all to themselves, while the Flirt, Little Fleta, Hesper and Bossier sent their greetings from their snug quarters at the boneyard. Along the grand thoroughfare might have been seen four or five drays and a go-cart or two, but even these apparently had nothing to do. If they did they had a very poor way of showing it. In the early part of the day, while the sun shone down hot, the sidewalk was almost entirely deserted, and it was only now and then that a poor devil could be seen skooting from one house to another, apparently on very urgent business. Certainly nothing short of that would have brought anyone out. We have our opinion of a man who would take a turn for

Locomotives have replaced the steamboats, but the Red River's presence is still felt.

pleasure along the landing these hot days. In the afternoon as the shades of evening draw near, the sidewalks could certainly boast of a multitude of idlers who lounged about on barrels, boxes, etc., discussing the news of the day, and swapping stale jokes and attempts at witticism. There were cattle men, gentlemen, and men of all kinds shooting their mouths off on almost all topics that did not require the use of common sense. Now and then a sensible remark was made but it fell unheeded and wasted itself on the desert air. Thus passed the dullest day of the season and long may it be before we see its duplicate.

The river men, still fighting the change, thought restricted river traffic was the result of stringent laws which discouraged people from investing in steamboats. Rate-cutting at competing points was a problem, of course, but only one of many. Ships had to be constructed in accordance with the dimensions of the railroad bridges, which was not always the most economical method. These same bridges, the river men claimed, obstructed river traffic and caused high insurance rates.

The river business was heavily regulated by legislation, too. All boats had to be registered and licensed, with a $500 fine for transporting freight or persons without a license (and half the fine going to the informant!). If the president of the company, in whose name the license was filed, were to die, a new license was required. An oath of ownership must be filed. And early in the 1820s, the Legislature of Mississippi passed a tax on boats arriving in Natchez from out of state, in order to secure funds for the maintenance of a hospital there. The tax was three to five dollars per boat, depending on her size, with each officer and boat band taxed fifty cents. Congress refused to approve this measure, but it was evidence enough to the river men that they were being exploited!

According to law, separate inspections of the hulls and boilers had to be carried out, the former every twelve months, the latter every six months. Each inspection cost five dollars. Since inspection of the copper boilers involved testing them with three times their ordinary pressure, steamboat owners screamed. Such testing every six months would be ruinous, they cried, with the strain causing leaks at the rivets and rendering boilers useless.

The presence of a sufficient number of skilled engineers was required on board, or the steamboat owner was held responsible for any damage to property or passengers by explosion or derangement of engine machinery. If any person was killed through the captain's misconduct, negligence, or inattention to duties, such captain was considered guilty of manslaughter, unless he could prove otherwise. This provision included death from an explosion or other injurious escape of steam.

Early Red River bridges were built by the railroads and shared by other traffic.

The handwriting was on the wall, and everyone recognized it as the railroad's work. By the late 1880s, railway companies were being chartered right and left, building feeder lines throughout the Red River Valley and continuing to drain off river business. In 1882 the New Orleans Pacific Railway reached Shreveport, seven years after its charter. By 1884 the Vicksburg, Shreveport and Pacific was completed, having fallen heir to most of the name and the eastern part of the old Vicksburg, Shreveport and Texas right of way. The Vicksburg, Shreveport and Pacific Railroad then proceeded to build the first bridge over the Red River. Later, the New Orleans Pacific was consolidated into the Texas and Pacific corporate structure, and the Vicksburg, Shreveport and Pacific became part of today's Illinois Central.

In 1883 the Gulf, Shreveport and Kansas City Railroad Company was incorporated. By 1885 its line reached forty miles away to Logansport on the Sabine River. Along the way, it trimmed its goals and its corporate image, changing its name to the Shreveport-Houston Railway. Sold under foreclosure in 1890, it was changed once again to the Houston and Shreveport Railway Company, and by the turn of the century the connecting lines were absorbed into a resurrected giant, the Southern Pacific.

Shreveport's first direct rail route to Little Rock and on to the Upper Midwest was provided by the St. Louis, Arkansas and Southern Line in 1888. In 1887 the seeds of the Kansas City Southern were sown as the Kansas City Suburban Belt Railroad was organized, only to be reorganized in 1893 as the Kansas City, Pittsburgh and Gulf Railroad. Finally, it became the familiar Kansas City Southern. Backed in its southward expansion by Holland's royal family, two of the towns on the old KCS route, DeQueen and Mena, were named for the reigning monarch of the time, Queen Wilhelmena. The KCS was in Shreveport by 1897, providing the city with long rail connections to all points north, south, east and west.

Two other railway lines were important in the history of the river-rail controversy. William Buchanan built a short private railroad to haul logs from the south to his lumber mill at Stamps, Arkansas; this line later became the Louisiana and Arkansas railroad. Its tracks eventually stretched north to Hope, Arkansas, and south to Alexandria.

William Edenborn, the first president of American Steel and Wire Company, organized and owned the Shreveport and Red River Valley Railroad, chartered in 1896. Beginning modestly with a stretch of track from Shreveport to Coushatta, it had reached Alexandria by 1902. In 1903 Edenborn organized the Louisiana Railroad and Navigation Company, which purchased all the properties of the Shreveport and Red River Valley Railroad, and extended the line to New Orleans. The first through service from Shreveport to New Orleans was offered by the line in 1906, and was unique in that, from the time of its incorporation, it had been owned lock, stock and barrel by a single individual!

In 1928 the railway properties were bought from both the estates of Buchanan and Edenborn, and merged into the Louisiana and Arkansas Railway Company, which survives today as an affiliate of the Kansas City Southern.

The majority of the steamboats, of course, were long gone, with a few ships still plying their lonely way at the turn of the century. The Red River

Line proved to be one of the hardiest, with the *W.T. Scovell* carrying on the grand old steamer tradition even as late as 1911.

It is said that there have been three major economic developments that have greatly affected the history of northwest Louisiana. The first was the removal of the Great Raft; the second was the coming of the railroads; the third was the discovery of oil and gas. Nothing, however, so directly affected the fate of the Red River as the railroad's arrival. The steaming, spitting, iron monsters whose gleaming tracks soon crisscrossed the entire valley spelled the end of the river's dominant role in the area, and the dawn of a new era.

Bossier City Grows Up

Emerging from the shadow of a "big brother" has never been easy. The shadow lengthens, grows, and towers, always somehow seeming to eclipse the smaller of the two. Located directly across the Red River from Shreveport, Bossier City struggled for years to capture its own spotlight; recent history has allowed it the chance to step out of Shreveport's shadow into its own place in the sun.

Before the Vicksburg, Shreveport and Pacific Railroad built the first bridge across the Red River in 1884, the citizens of tiny Cane City (as Bossier was once called) had to ferry across the river for most of their needs. Originally named Bennett's Bluff, the sleepy city reflected its size in the two small stores located on the banks of the Red—Cane's and Bennett's. The name was later changed to Cane City, carrying this title until 1905, when Governor N.C. Blanchard chartered it as a village.

General Pierre Evatiste John Baptiste Bossier, a Natchitoches Congressman, was instrumental in having Bossier Parish created by an Act of the State Legislature on February 24, 1843. In September, 1882, the parish voted on the proposed removal of the parish seat from Bellevue to either Cane City or Benton. While the vote favored Cane City, a flaw in the 1879 constitution was later found, causing an act of the legislature to move the parish seat to its present location in Benton.

By 1907 the population had grown enough for the initially tiny village to be incorporated as the town of Bossier City. Its first city hall was a unique structure built by Bossier Mayor E.M. Hoyer with $1,150 from his own private account. The town later reimbursed Hoyer for the two-story building, when sufficient funds were accumulated. In 1926, the city constructed a new City Hall at a cost of $50,000. And in 1951, with a population in excess of 15,000, Governor Earl K. Long issued a proclamation making Bossier City a city!

Bossier was originally governed by the commission form of government, consisting of three commissioners, one of whom served as mayor. In July, 1977, a new form of government, strong mayor-council, was established due to the city's rapid growth.

During the last twenty-six years, the population of Bossier City has expanded from 15,740 to 55,000. Now the seventh largest city in Louisiana, it was designated the fastest-growing city in North Louisiana by the Census Report of 1970. Directing this growth all along has been the job of an active planning commission, working from a master plan for development adopted many years ago, with zoning provided for the metropolitan area. With approximately fifteen thousand homes, the city has a sufficient, yet not overabundant supply of housing. Choice building sites are plentiful, both within the city and near the suburbs, allowing for increased demand.

Part of the secret of Bossier City's rapid growth has been Barksdale Air Force Base, located in part within the city limits. Named after Lieutenant Eugene H. Barksdale, a World War I ace who died while flight testing an observation plane in 1926, the base was constructed from 1931-33, with the actual dedication on February 2, 1933. Air Training Command Headquarters was located on the base following World War II; after the outbreak of the Korean conflict, the Strategic Air Command (SAC) expanded rapidly and chose Barksdale as one of its key bases.

Barksdale Air Force Base in 1936

The first SAC planes to fly out of Barksdale were B-29 Stratofortresses. A newer and faster jet bomber, the B-47 Stratojet replaced the old B-29s in 1953, bringing with it KC-97 Stratotankers, SAC's "flying filling station." This, in turn, was replaced by the KC-135 Jet Stratotanker, and the B-47 was succeeded by the eight jet engine B-52 Super Stratofortress, the world's largest bomber and airborne missile launcher.

Covering 22,000 acres and encompassing an area some five miles wide by nine and a half miles long, the military installation has both command and operational roles. The land on which the base is located was purchased by citizens of the local community and donated to the government for the specific purpose of establishing a permanent military installation.

Barksdale Air Force Base is the home of the Second Bombardment Wing, responsible for the base's major mission, as well as its many support organizations. Other specialized tenant organizations are also based here, among them the Headquarters of the Eighth Air Force, one of two numbered commands of the Strategic Air Command Force. The base's population is 7,331 military and civilian personnel, with an annual payroll of $86,246,000. Many of Barksdale's military retirees return to make Bossier City their permanent home.

The city itself has grown into a viable entity on its own, a metropolis capable of supporting every facet of city life. Recreation is an important part of this life, with programs directed by the city recreational department, the YMCA, local churches, and the parish school system. In addition, Bossier residents can make use of swimming pools, tennis courts, parks, recreational buildings, lighted ball fields, and gymnasiums. Palmetto Country Club and Eastwood Country Club provide excellent golf, swimming pools, and club facilities. And with three large lakes in the immediate vicinity, plus several others within easy driving distance, Bossierites have many opportunities for fishing, swimming and boating.

Bossier Parish schools have attained a level of education far surpassing most cities of its size; in fact, the Educational Resource Center media program was rated the best in the nation in 1973. This computer program is well recognized within the state and is currently helping other parish school systems. In addition, the Apollo Elementary school in Bossier has received national attention with its innovative experimental facilities and techniques.

Being located in the heart of the rich Red River Valley is extremely conducive to agricultural production, and Bossier City is no exception. Like Shreveport, for many years its chief agricultural product was cotton, but recent years have seen a wide diversity of products develop, including soy beans, corn, hay, forest and cattle. And while agriculture continues to hold its own economic importance to the city, commerce and industry are playing ever-increasing roles as Bossier continues to develop.

As the young country and western stars of the forties and fifties rode the crest of stardom, buoyed by the nationally-famous Louisiana Hayride, so now the rising stars of the seventies have their chance. Hayride USA, the Louisiana Hayride's successor, stages its well-renowned show in Bossier City, with top names appearing week after week.

Louisiana Downs Race Track has been one of the city's largest drawing cards, with approximately 800,000 people pouring into Bossier each year,

Bossier City's Louisiana Downs is one of the nation's finest horseracing facilities.

and annual increases expected. Its 100-day thoroughbred racing season attracts visitors from neighboring states, providing a tremendous boost to the city's economy.

"A city small enough to care, large enough to serve" is Bossier City's motto. From sleepy Cane City to hustling, bustling Bossier City, finally, it has stepped out of Shreveport's shadow and into its own place of well-deserved prominence.

The Recent Past

Bridges

A river is such a natural physical boundary that it often divides two entirely different types of people. Settlers on one side of the river, having little or no contact with settlers on the other side, tend to develop in varied and diverse ways, often with lifestyles, habits and even languages at distinct odds. "Bridging" that gap is no easy task; dozens of present-day structures, and ghosts of bridges past, stand silent and majestic witness to the schism created by the river.

Until the late 1800s, the Red River divided Shreve Town from a tiny settlement called Cane City. As the first connecting span, the now-defunct Vicksburg, Shreveport and Pacific Bridge was built across the water in 1884, sleepy Cane City began to grow. Partially as a result of the increased ease of access, the little city was incorporated in 1907, and re-named Bossier City.

The Vicksburg, Shreveport and Pacific Bridge was the first permanent traffic structure to cross the Red River. Located near the present-day Civic Center, where the Illinois Central Gulf railroad bridge now stands, it was a combination vehicular traffic and railroad bridge, constructed at a total cost of $300,000. The wooden structure served as the final link for the Vicksburg, Shreveport and Pacific Railway into the city. Its location, however, was quite a controversial issue; so much so, in fact, that the city gave the railroad the right of way through the middle of downtown Shreveport to gain the desired location. The railroad had originally requested a location near Fort Humbug, currently the Veterans Administration Hospital and Veterans Park area.

In order to allow foot, wagon, and vehicular traffic to cross the Red River, wooden platforms were laid over the bridge's railroad crossties. A toll was collected from travelers on both sides of the bridge. In 1916, the Vicksburg, Shreveport and Pacific Bridge was replaced by a steel monolith owned by the Illinois Central Gulf Railroad. Both bridges featured spans which could pivot, allowing boats to pass. Gasoline powered machinery, housed in little structures mounted on the bridge, was used to turn the spans automatically.

Although the machinery that turned the spans is no longer used, it is conceivable that the Illinois Central Gulf Bridge could be turned by hand today. In order for the spans to pivot, the tracks must be disconnected, and a large "key" inserted into the pivoting mechanism. The mechanism could be turned by men walking around the machinery with key in hand similar to the action of winding a watch. Many years ago, these special bridges with pivoting spans were essential, having to be opened regularly for dredging boats dispatched by the Corps of Engineers.

July 23, 1890, witnessed a freak accident on the railroad drawbridge leading into Shreveport. The Vicksburg, Shreveport and Pacific passenger train signalled for the bridge just at the moment that the *E.G. Wheelock*, a steamboat, also signalled. The draw was opened for the steamer, but Monk, the engineer, found his locomotive uncontrollable and in less than a minute, the locomotive leaped into Red River with the tender, leaving the train proper on the track. Who blew the whistle first was never known, but it was the subject of bitter dispute for months thereafter.

Currently, in addition to the bridges that span the waterway, there is a free ferry in use on the Red west of Bradley, Arkansas.

The first bridge built entirely for vehicular traffic was the old Traffic Street Bridge, dedicated in 1915. In addition to providing an additional means of access to Bossier City, it also supported various utility lines crossing the river. Connecting Lake Street to Barksdale Boulevard, the old structure was then a toll bridge, charging five cents for pedestrians and twenty-five cents for teams or automobiles. Confederate war veterans were favored in the hiring of toll collectors. The tolls ended in the 1920s, and rails were added for streetcar traffic. In 1955, the bridge was closed to all but walkers, and in June, 1968, the old Traffic Street Bridge was demolished. The Long-Allen Bridge, better known as the Texas Street Bridge, was the second vehicular bridge built over the Red River. Completed in 1934 at a total cost of $788,000, it spanned the river at the foot of Texas Street, standing even now as a vital traffic artery.

In 1957, the 2,700 foot Broadmoor-Barksdale Bridge was constructed. Its first year of construction, 1953, saw a spell of abnormally wet weather cause a sudden fifteen-foot rise in the river, toppling a vital supporting pier. Plagued by troubles throughout its construction, the $3.5 million structure was later re-named the Shreveport-Barksdale Bridge. A second span was added in 1973, at a cost of $4 million for the bridge itself, and an additional $1 million for the approaches.

The successor to the Old Traffic Street Bridge, the expressway bridge over Red River, was built as part of the I-20 Caddo project. Begun in January, 1960, the construction was completed in 1965.

Of all the traffic arteries between Shreveport and Bossier, perhaps none has been so controversial as the Seventieth Street, or "Jimmie Davis" Bridge. Contrary to master plans drawn up by both the cities of Shreveport and Bossier, the bridge was planned at a point near then-Governor Jimmie Davis' property in Bossier Parish. The Davis-approved plans showed a two-lane approach to the bridge from U.S. 71 bisecting Governor Davis' property. During the waning days of Davis' term, several support piers of the bridge were constructed, to insure its location there. The intent was obvious: said supports remained, idly standing for two years before bridge construction resumed. It was later discovered that the right of way from the west had not even been purchased yet. The Seventieth Street Bridge was completed in 1970, at a total cost of $3.8 million.

And so they stand: traffic arteries between Shreveport and Bossier City, between Caddo and Bossier Parish; mute observers of, and participants in, the colorful history of the Red River. Each has a story to tell, a slice of a particular time to relate to, a link with the past. And each has been a vital part of the yet-unwinding story of the Big Red.

Navigation

Breaking the Red River to harness as a dependable waterway has been no easy task in the past, nor does it promise to be in the future. With the demise of the steamboat and the growth of the railroad, the river itself has not really been used as a viable transportation route since the early 1900s. The subject of much controversy, navigation on Red River would require the accomplishment of at least three corrective steps:

1. A channel deep enough to accommodate barges and tugboats would have to be found or dredged along the Red's sandy bottom, then marked by buoys.
2. The Red's bad habit of shifting sandbars around on its bed, so as to make last week's charts obsolete next week, would have to be cured.
3. The level of the river water, which in its present untamed state ranges from flood to trickle, depending on the season and the uncertain rainfall in its drainage basin, must be averaged out to a workable year-round norm.

Given the attainment of these three objectives, navigation on the Red River would connect Shreveport and other cities along the river with 29,000 inland navigable waterways. Because the Red is connected to the Mississippi via Old River, restoration of navigation would allow local industry and commerce direct access to the deepwater ports of Baton Rouge and New Orleans to the south, and to the north, the shallow draft navigation system of the Mississippi above Baton Rouge and to the Arkansas, Missouri, Ohio, Illinois, Tennessee and Cumberland shallow draft systems.

The issue of restoring navigation on the Red River did not crop up overnight. Over a thousand acres of valuable farmland are devoured annually by receding banks in the Mississippi River to Shreveport stretch of the Red River Valley alone. The estimated economic loss, based on land value, potential revenue from crops and pastureland, and destruction of levees and other structures, is over $12.5 million per year. It soon became evident through these losses that bank stabilization was necessary to prevent caving shores from eating away the valuable lands adjacent to the river and to provide a stable channel for navigation.

Therefore, the Red River Valley Association was founded in 1926, to coordinate the efforts of civic leaders, businessmen, and farmers throughout the area in lobbying for restoration of navigation. Comprised of 120 members from four states, the organization gained support from local congressional delegations and from national legislators who recognized the Red River's potential for renewal as a major transportation artery.

The first president of the Association was George Hearne, a local Shreveport merchant. His election was significant in that it expressed the mercantile interest in navigation: to establish some controls against the unpredictable flooding which destroyed people's buying power, and to seek permanent re-establishment of navigation in order to achieve more competitive freight rates. The methodology of the Association in taking

Tugboat and barges on the Red. At present, Red River navigation is a sometime thing.

action on a problem was to shape an idea into a project, then justify the project to the federal government. If the government approved of the idea, the U.S. Corps of Engineers would be called in to make a study of the proposed project. After the completion of the study, Congress must then approve.

In 1944 the first major flood control project sponsored by the Association bore fruit. Denison Dam, authorized by Congress in 1938, was constructed as a flood control measure. A $77,500,000 project, it served as a bulwark against flood waters from almost forty thousand square miles of the upper Red River watershed.

But flooding was not the only problem dealt with by the Association. Members in Arkansas, Oklahoma and Texas argued that, indeed, they had too *little* water; reservoirs were needed in those areas. And so the organization continued to deal with the water concerns of its members, meeting for two days every April to plan its annual strategy.

In 1969, $20,899,000 was appropriated through Congressional approval for projects of prime concern to the Red River Valley Association. Of this appropriation, $4.5 million was earmarked for projects in Louisiana. In addition, the efforts of the Association have helped to bring about tremendous federal and state expenditures for flood control, independent of the navigation issue.

Navigation as well as land use are hampered by uncertain water level, channel shifts and unstable banks. In this picture, the Red has eroded its right bank almost through to adjacent Cane River Lake, severing a farm road. Scrapped auto bodies have been brought to the site for use as bank protection.

Red River Waterway Project

An extensive study was made by the U.S. Corps of Engineers, based on the recommendations of the Red River Valley Association and other proponents of renewing navigation on the Red River. This study, known as the Red River Waterway Project, concerned the feasibility of once again transforming the river into a viable transportation artery. The basic purposes of its scope were to examine the costs, time and effort involved in navigation, and bank stabilization.

Senator J. Bennett Johnston called the Red River Waterway "the economic salvation of a very, very poor area." President Jimmy Carter threatened in 1977 to discontinue it, along with a number of other public works projects. Its proponents argue fiercely for its benefits, its critics utilize every opportunity to point out its flaws. One of the largest projects ever undertaken by the U.S. Army Corps of Engineers, it is second only to the Tennessee-Tombigbee Waterway in Mississippi and Alabama, a project which is expected to cost several hundred million dollars more. It has remained since its conception one of the most controversial projects ever embarked upon in this area. And even now, the controversy rages.

Pros

The intent of the Red River Waterway Project is to provide a navigable route from the Mississippi River via Old River to Shreveport. This involves constructing a 9 by 200 foot navigation channel, with five locks and dams and related bank stabilization from the Mississippi River to Shreveport. By cutting channels through the many curves and meanders of the Red River, the Corps of Engineers hopes to straighten the river's course and create oxbow lakes in the cutoffs. This realigned channel will be 236 miles in length upon completion, and will be generally confined within the limits of the existing river channel.

One of the major purposes of the project is to halt the continuing loss, because of the river's meandering, of valuable lands, and the improvements located upon these lands. In addition, the project will provide a dependable channel for shallow draft navigation, adding to the diversity of the transportation system in the region. A reduction of flood damages would naturally occur as the result of improved bank stabilization, and existing flood protection works. Maintenance costs on these flood protection works would be reduced, and the water of the river itself enhanced for municipal, industrial and agricultural use.

Positive effects of the project include the development of new recreation facilities at lock and dam sites, at selected sites along the navigation channel, and at oxbow lakes formed by channel realignment. In addition to these expanded facilities, the fishery habitat should greatly improve. Reduced land losses, transportation savings and increased recreational opportunities will all add to the national and regional income of the area.

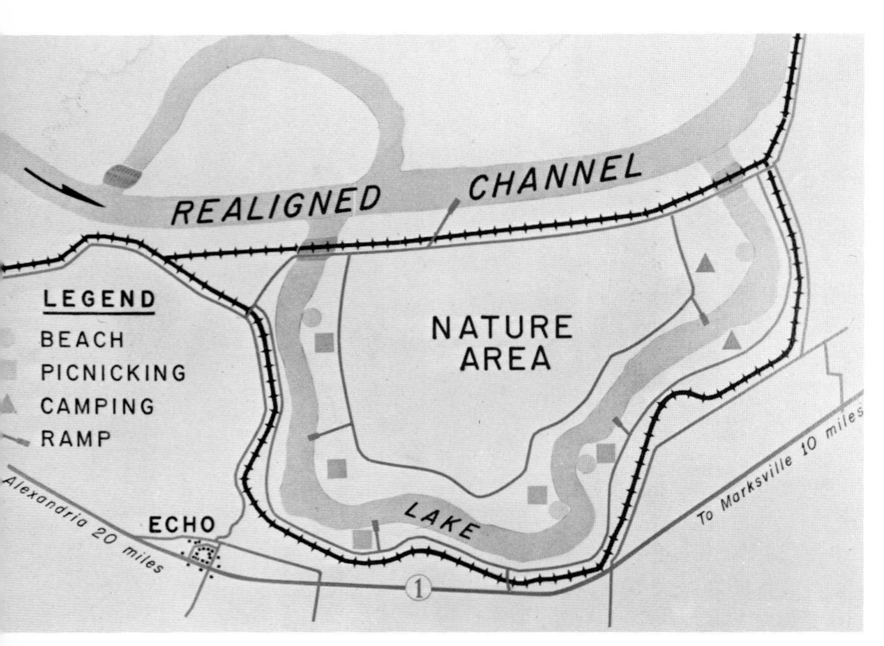

Completion of the Red River Waterway Project would involve straightening of the river's channel, with the resulting oxbow lakes devoted to recreational use.

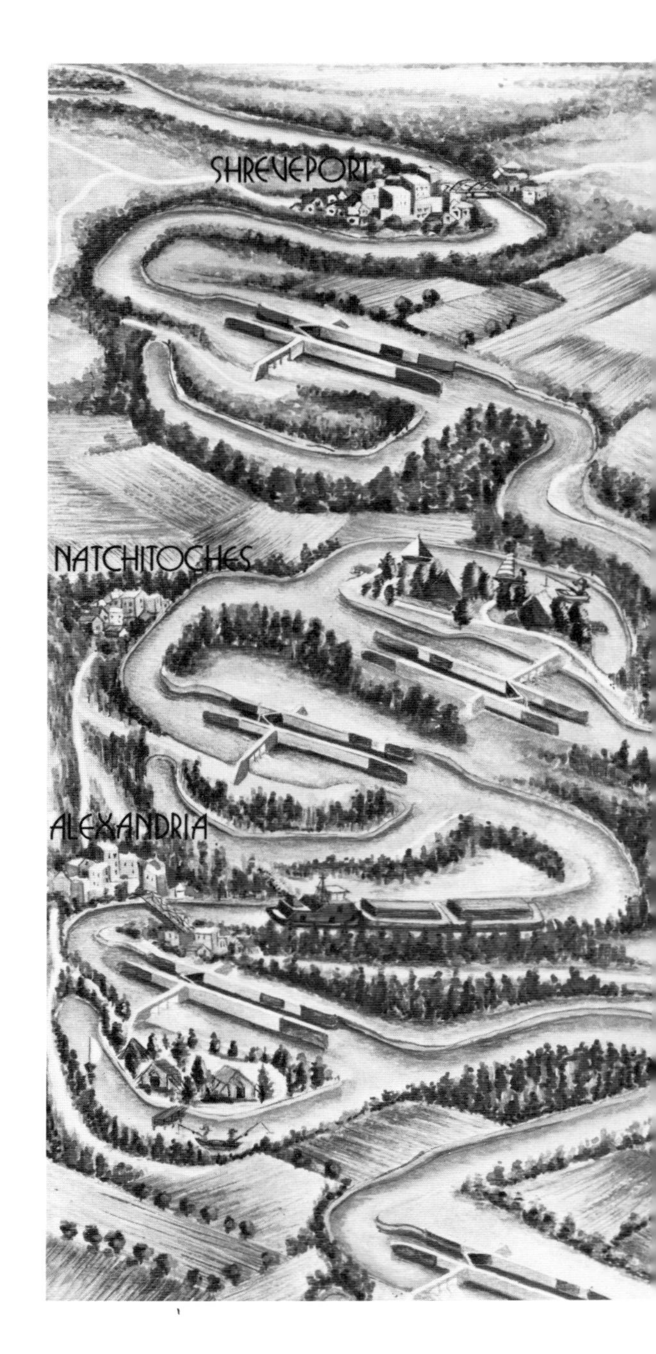

Four major park developments are planned near the channel. A 900 acre site is planned near Echo, a 1,200 acre site one mile upstream from Boyce, a 1,360 acre site thirteen miles downstream from Shreveport, and a 990 acre site three miles downstream from Shreveport. These parks will also involve the construction of increased access roads, parking areas, launching ramps, picnic and camping facilities, water and sanitary facilities, and swimming areas. In addition to these four large public parks, thirty smaller park developments are planned throughout the area.

Over the fifty-year project life, sufficient jobs should be created to support a gain in population roughly comparable to a city the size of Alexandria. Economic activity, however, should exceed this population gain because of a higher labor force participation rate and more efficient resource utilization. The project will also create a change in land use patterns; more land, especially in Shreveport and Alexandria, should be committed to urban-type usage than ever before.

The long-range results of the Red River Waterway Project have been outlined by the U.S. Corps of Engineers in their final report to Congress. Basically, these results are broken down into thirteen benefits to the area:

1. Increase in commerce movement over the waterway. Some 5,706,000 tons of annual bulk movement are projected to utilize the newly navigable river.
2. Erosion prevention. Bank stabilization will prevent the annual loss of approximately 1,060 acres and the revenue derived from this land.
3. Flood control benefits. Improvement of flood protection works will prevent damage to the levee systems, railroads, highways, bridges, pipelines, powerlines, communication lines and buildings.
4. Flood damage reduction. Over 40,000 acres of cleared land will be saved from flood damage. Intensified agricultural production may be implemented on 56,710 acres of cleared land and 6,680 acres of forest land.
5. Irrigation. Slack water pools will be provided to be used for irrigating 11,800 acres of agricultural lands.
6. Less water treatment required. Maintaining the river stages at higher levels will result in a reduction in treatment requirements for 20.8 million gallons a day by the year 2025.
7. Employment benefits. Increased job opportunities will be available during construction and maintenance of the project.
8. Increased recreation opportunities. Some 6,080 acres of public lakes and 10,900 acres of recreational lands adjacent to the navigation channel are planned. The average annual general recreation attendance is projected to be 2,670,000 visitors.
9. Induced industrial development. In addition to encouraging the growth of manufacturing and related service industries, a navigable waterway will greatly facilitate the marketing of the area's

agricultural products, such as its expanding soybean crops. Industrial development should be more pronounced in Shreveport and Alexandria.

10. Establishment of more small manufacturing firms. Because of transportation advantages and favorable industrial sites, more small manufacturing firms will look at Louisiana as a future location.
11. Reduced maintenance costs. Existing bank stabilization works will require less maintenance.
12. Higher wage rates, a broadened tax base, and enhanced property values will result from the renewal of navigation.
13. Increased security from levee crevasses and attending flood losses will occur.

According to the Corps of Engineers, the only adverse impacts to be felt are the loss or alteration of 43,100 acres of land. Of this land, 8,250 acres would be permanently lost (physically removed or excavated). In order to facilitate the project, five highway and four railroad bridges crossing the waterway will require renovation or replacement.

One ironic note: after the completion of the navigation project, the Red River would become more green than red, due to slower-flowing water which would no longer keep river-bottom sand and silt in suspension.

Cons

According to critics of the project, the list of adverse effects is indeed longer than the list of benefits. The cost of the project increased over 400 percent in ten years. When the waterway was first authorized by Congress in 1968, its construction carried a $239 million price tag. By 1976, that figure had increased to $897.6 million, and by early 1979, the total figure had topped the $1 billion mark. Of this amount, the federal government's final share is expected to be $1.04 billion, and the state's share $51.1 million, raised from a 2-mill tax levied by the Red River Waterway Commission.

According to C.W. Shelton, special assistant to the chief of the engineering division for the Red River Waterway, the increase is accounted for in large part by inflation. But, say critics, much of the increase also stems from alterations in project plans.

The Corps of Engineers took a totally new look at the project in 1971. Then, in 1976, two years after funding by Congress, the Corps came up with an advanced engineering design. As a result of this re-evaluation, the cost also advanced from $514 million to $870 million. The benefit-to-cost ratio fell from $1.20 in benefits to every $1.00 spent, to $1.06 in benefits to every $1.00 spent.

Initial survey estimates by the Corps were based on a variety of sources, but mostly they relied on two methods: comparison of costs incurred in similar projects, and use of estimates based on cursory designs of planned structures. It has been charged that the utilization of these survey

COSTS AND BENEFITS	
Annual Charges	
Interest (at 3¼%)	$35,445,000
Amortization	5,739,000
Maintenance	8,643,000
Replacements	160,000
Loss of land	699,000
Fish and wildlife losses	44,000
Groundwater losses	282,000
Total	$51,012,000
Annual Benefits	
Prevention of damage to levees	1,565,000
Prevention of damage to utility	3,756,000
Prevention of destruction of land	2,515,000
Elimination of bank cave-ins	1,255,000
Less frequent flooding	320,000
Reduced maintenance of revetments	2,103,000
Security against levee crevasses	194,000
Irrigation	14,000
Reduced cost of water supply	19,000
Reduced sedimentation	143,000
Fish and wildlife	115,000
Recreation	4,071,000
Area redevelopment	8,554,000
Navigation	29,457,000
Total	$54,081,000

Benefit-to-cost Ratio: 1.06 to 1
(Figures supplied by U.S. Army Corps of Engineers, N.O. District)

estimates as the basis for authorizing and funding the project by Congress was incorrect. Critics of the project believe that more detailed engineering studies should have been made.

Also adding to the cost of the project is the fact that the interest rate charged on project funds is based on the 3 ¼ percent rate current at the time of the survey—not the higher rate current at the time of project funding.

The Corps of Engineers assumes for their projections that shippers will switch to barge traffic from another mode of transportation, primarily because of possible savings in freight rates. These savings have been questioned, on the basis of the fact that it is difficult to get accurate rates for railroad freight, currently the cheapest mode of transportation, without access to their books. In addition, the Corps has projected theoretical barge rates whose accuracy has been questioned.

The estimated savings in transportation is also based on the assumption that the project will be fully operational within the first year, and that there will be a high frequency of use of the new waterway. Project critics allege that a gradual transition to river traffic is more likely. In addition, if plants locate in industrial parks around the port sites, they say, the business of trucking and rail firms will be enhanced.

Proponents believe the waterway is well worth the price in light of the economic and recreational benefits that will accrue. Senators Russell Long and J. Bennett Johnston, along with other members of the Louisiana congressional delegation, have stressed the potential value of the waterway for years.

According to Senator Johnston, "Regional economic gain is the most important reason this project is justified. In the factories, the industrial plants, the distribution plants that are going to be drawn to this area . . . as a result of Red River navigation. Think of the fuel you can save by navigation on this Red River—by gasoline truck it takes 16 miles per gallon for a ton of freight, 54 per diesel truck, railroad gets 178, and water-borne carriers, 306 miles per gallon."

Former U.S. Representative Joe D. Waggonner encouraged the public to look deeper than simply the obvious costs. "Don't just look at the benefit-cost ratio. Look at secondary or induced benefits. Here is where the bonanza really is. These benefits could be, and more often than not are, as much as twenty or thirty times the direct benefits, if the track record of other projects holds true here."

Senator Long pointed out the indirect energy benefits that would accrue with the waterway's construction. "There is a lot of lignite in this area which we will necessarily have to use to meet our energy requirements during the next thirty years. This Red River Waterway is a logical way to move that heavy material."

Given the fact that Shreveport, Alexandria and Natchitoches owe their very existence to the river's former commercial capabilities, it is not surprising that resurrecting navigation on the Red should be a natural step in the future. After all, utilizing the river for the benefit of this area is hardly a new idea, having once before brought prosperity to the communities along its shores.

And while the public balances the pros and cons of renewed navigation, the Red River flows placidly, muddily along, oblivious to all but the centuries of rich history behind it.

Increased flood protection is a benefit of the proposed project that would be welcomed by residents of the Red River Valley.

Modern History

Big Red has begun to come full circle. Where rats once scurried among the forgotten ruins of deserted warehouses, renovated businesses now stand. Where dark alleyways and unsavory characters once made it unsafe for ladies to walk, parkway floodlights now illuminate the night. Where crumbling buildings and unmown fields once stood, now stand new restaurants, office buildings, night clubs, and shops. After years of degeneration, the Red River and its frontage land are once again taking their place as a focal point of the City's growth and activity . . . from back street to front again.

In 1957, Bossier City approved a $3,500,000 bond issue to use the Red River as a source of its water supply. This landmark vote came after years of depending on Shreveport for its water, and it now makes Bossier the only city in the area which draws its municipal water from the river. In 1959, its water treatment plant and distribution system were in full operation, and Big Red was on its way to becoming an increasingly important factor in city life.

While the early and mid-1900s had seen the evolution of Shreveport's riverfront into a rundown, semi-desolate area, the 1960s saw its transition from the "batture" to rejuvenated central city. The restoration of navigation was promised, and new life was breathed into an otherwise forgotten part of the city.

The redevelopment of the riverfront followed the approval in 1961 of a bond issue for the completion, furnishing and equipping of the Civic Theater, improving the riverfront and the erection of a convention hall. The Civic Theater was dedicated in 1965, paving the way to attract large events, formerly held in other parts of the city, down to the river's edge. In addition, the modern theater provides a contemporary backdrop, complete with the latest in acoustic and lighting innovations, for touring attractions that might otherwise pass Shreveport by. Utilized for gala, spectacular happenings year-round, the Civic Theater serves as the focal point for nighttime riverfront activity. The spectacular forty foot illuminated fountain erected in front of the theater was contributed to the city by Southwestern Electric Power Company.

Also standing regally in front of the Civic Theater is a monument to Captain Henry Miller Shreve, dedicated June 10, 1976. The nine-foot statue, sculpted by Arthur C. Morgan, rests on a red granite base. More than one thousand contributions were made for the $25,000 statue fundraising effort. On hand for the unveiling of the inspiring piece were seven direct descendants of Captain Shreve.

In 1965, Shreveport called on the services of City Planner Arch Winter to evaluate the city's needs. After studying the economic supports, growth potentials and space needs of downtown Shreveport, Winter put together a booklet that called for revitalizing the area. His recommendations include the planning of more green, park-like areas within the central business district, and the construction of a Red River marina to breathe new life into the riverfront.

Captain Shreve

Shreveport Civic Center

During the sixties and seventies a riverfront development called Shreve Square blossomed, wilted slightly, then blossomed anew as new businesses came and went, but several cornerstone establishments remained. Utilizing renovated buildings in the area under the Texas Street Bridge, the atmosphere is decidedly quaint; old walls were knocked out, windows re-glassed, fresh paint applied, and voila! . . . the emergence of a tiny rebuilt city-within-a-city. Restaurants, night clubs, specialty shops, and clothing stores now mix with century-old warehouses and produce companies, as old gracefully blends with new.

In late 1969 former U.S. Representative Waggonner, Senator Long and the late Senator Allen J. Ellender announced a federal urban renewal grant of $1,761,126, made to provide three-fourths of the $2.3 million needed for revitalization of the riverfront. The work began in mid-1970; the remaining one-fourth of the fund was provided by one of twelve propositions approved in a capital improvements bond issue in 1968.

Included in the same proposition was half the cost of a botanical gardens and art center on the River Parkway. The remainder of the cost of the complex, to be known as the Barnwell Memorial Cultural Center, was in the form of a gift of $250,000, donated by the family of the late R.S. (Cap) Barnwell. Embracing the best of both worlds, the Barnwell Center offers museum and exhibition space, as well as meeting areas; a large domed Conservatory houses lush and exotic plant life.

Long planned as a vital transportation alternative, the Clyde Fant Parkway was constructed and named after a beloved former mayor of Shreveport. Connecting Broadmoor with downtown, the Parkway begins under the Shreveport-Barksdale Bridge and parallels the river all the way to the Barnwell Center.

When construction was planned for the Parkway, recreational facilities were added along its route. Veterans Park is a unique playground area with

Stripped of façades and sandblasted, architectural beauties of the 1800s now house shopping, dining and entertainment establishments in Shreve Square.

Barnwell Conservatory

innovative equipment that encourages children to use their imagination in play. Veterans Park Amphitheater, a large, simple wooden outdoor structure that rests beside a miniature lake, is used to showcase outdoor concerts, plays, and civic efforts in a rustic setting.

Perhaps one of the most popular of the parkway additions has been the bicycle trail. Running alongside the river for a distance of some five miles, the bike trail attracts young and old alike, its narrow paved road winding through cool forest areas and riverfront scenery. The trail was constructed on both sides of the Parkway, so that riders may cross under the highway to the other side and bicycle, jog or walk either way. Within the wide expanse of middle ground between the north and south bound lanes is a brightly lit frisbee golf course, another popular family attraction.

In 1976 the Shreveport Bicentennial Commission, in conjunction with the Junior League, a women's service organization, began an annual tradition that has become more popular with every passing year. The Red River Revel, a festival for the arts, was conceived as a Bicentennial gift to the city. Its purpose was to create a festival that would provide an umbrella for the

Red
River
Revel

This scenic bicycle trail along Clyde Fant Parkway in Shreveport borders the river for five miles.

arts; a celebration that would "bring the arts to everyone," young and old, rich and poor alike. In so doing, the Red River Revel's secondary purpose was also achieved: to bring people back downtown, specifically, back to the Red River, where the city's real life began.

Held on the banks of the river around the Barnwell Center and Civic Theater, the Revel was judged "Shreveport's Best Ad" in 1977, and in 1978 it attracted in excess of three hundred thousand visitors. For seven days, generally around the first week in October, over eight hundred performers and musicians display their talents on three stages daily from 9 A.M. till 9 P.M. Artists and craftsmen travel to the Revel from a fifteen-state area to sell their handiwork. Food booths featuring the cuisine of different countries, multi-media presentations, classic films, children's face-painting, crafts demonstrations, plays, mini-workshops, concerts and dances are all part of this monumentally successful celebration of the arts. The price? Absolutely free to the public. Profits from the previous year's Revel are poured back into the following year's effort, along with a grant from the National Endowment for the arts for funding.

One of the highlights of the festival is the aesthetic education program for children. Each day two to three thousand fourth and fifth graders from both public and private schools are bussed in from Caddo and Bossier parishes to participate in the Revel. This practice exposes the greatest number of children possible to an excellent representative sampling of the arts.

The Red River Revel is one of many movements back toward the riverfront in modern times. Current city planning involves more and more planning around the river, instead of away from it. Architects and builders are beginning to see the once-neglected waterway as a potential source of usefulness and beauty, as well as the focus of a new direction in city design. The old becomes new, the past becomes future, and Big Red edges its way back toward the center of city life where it began.

Big Red's Potential

The genesis of Shreveport was in the swirling currents of the Red River; its story and the story of the city are inextricably entwined. In its infancy the city depended upon the river as a baby upon its mother, nourishing its fledgling businesses upon river commerce and transportation. And as a child grows to be independent and strong, Shreveport grew to stand firmly on its own commercial feet, despite the dwindling importance of the river.

Considered the "back yard" of the downtown area for many decades, Big Red originally sustained dozens of industries which thrived along its banks. Those same industries in recent years have relied almost solely upon rail access and trucking for their continued success. With the advent of navigation just over the horizon, the city is yet again turning to the river for sustenance. Big Red's potential is enormous, and the river's time has come!

Becoming the focal point for downtown Shreveport involves not only the renewal of navigation on the river, but also cleansing, beautifying, and re-developing the riverfront. The Central Business District Riverfront Development project, a complex of structures encompassing both commercial and social functions, states as its main objective the re-development of the riverfront for public use and enjoyment.

This urban design project found its beginnings in the recommendations of City Planner Arch Winter. Winter's proposal suggested a park development along the riverfront, designed with an urban character because of the density of public facilities in the area. The Shreveport Urban Renewal Agency has purchased the only remaining private land between Commerce Street and the river, to be used for re-development of that area.

An integral part of the project is the construction of the North-South Freeway, long proposed for the state. When completed, the freeway will relieve much of the thru-traffic now having to use Spring and Market streets. In addition, the reduction of traffic on the Parkway would allow for the design of both at-grade and overhead pedestrian crossings, essential to encouraging more pedestrian traffic in the area. Without the freeway, traffic would eventually overload the capacity of both Spring and Market streets, and particularly the Parkway, severely straining their capabilities.

The project plans utilize and expand upon the existing commercial development along the riverfront—in particular the Shreve Square area and along Texas Street west of Commerce Street, and the restaurant/entertainment development on the west side of Commerce Street. These developments are excellent examples of enterprises that have encouraged downtown renewal. By renovating existing old buildings and adapting the structures to private use, the city experiences the best possible kind of urban renewal.

In addition, most of the existing businesses in the Shreve Square and restaurant/entertainment area of the riverfront support evening activities, thus keeping people in the downtown area for longer periods of time. This aspect of downtown support, especially, can be a valuable asset in attracting future conventions to Shreveport.

By encouraging the planning of other developments like Shreve Square in different segments of the riverfront area, Shreveport will be encouraging its own renewal. The renovation and adaptation of old but sound structures is certainly feasible, and indeed desirable, taking into account the limited undeveloped space left available on the riverfront.

As a complement to cultural and convention functions, the city must promote the riverfront location of businesses which enhance both daytime and nighttime activities. Also in support of both the proposed Convention Center and the central business district, there is a need for both transient and permanent housing, including hotel, apartment, high rise and low rise condominium developments. This type of housing, plus more hotel/motel accommodations adjacent to the district, are the only notable gaps in an area that is otherwise well suited to renewal and renovation.

In what seems a rather eclectic mixture of purposes, the land use west of Commerce Street combines warehouses, retail, commercial, transient housing and business activities. This type of arrangement has, nonetheless, previously worked well in other cities, notably New Orleans and San Francisco, and should be encouraged in Shreveport.

Strollers through the downtown area are concentrated mainly in an east-west direction along Texas Street. More pedestrian traffic throughout the riverfront area is desirable, as crowds of people seem to draw crowds of people. However, real reasons for people to walk from the central business district down to the river must be provided; there must also be places to house people on a twenty-four-hour basis. Further development of the private and public entertainment complexes on the riverfront demands that the entire area become a living, vital creation.

Conventions are, obviously, essential in drawing people to the riverfront as a focal point downtown. The planned Convention Center Complex will include exhibition space, meeting, dining and ballroom facilities. These facilities will be comprised of a 10,000 seat Coliseum, a 2,000-capacity Banquet Room/Ballroom, various suites of meeting rooms seating anywhere from 10 to 200, a 2,700 seat Theater/Auditorium, a 400 seat Intimate Theater, a 35,000 square foot Museum, a 78,000 square foot City Administration Office, and the addition of two domes to the Conservatory. The expansion of Barnwell Center in this way will allow it to better serve as a regional educational and tourist attraction.

In addition to these facilities, comfort stations are needed, as well as rentals and adequate parking.

Outdoor activities are an integral part of any people-oriented place. The rental of bicycles and outdoor games equipment, plus the provision of places for people to play and watch, will encourage these types of activities. Plazas, fountains, decks, vistas, walkways, boating access—all coupled with attractive landscaping—are a must throughout the entire Riverfront Complex.

There are endless varieties of ways in which to attract people to the riverfront area. In addition to conventions, there can be meetings of all kinds, specialized exhibits, art exhibits, small exclusive stores for shopping, lectures, lessons and rehearsals, ice skating, children's plays, unique restaurants, snack places, tourist information, theatre performances, open recitals, water shows, open exhibits for sculpture, sidewalk sales, farmers' markets, carnivals, fashion shows, circuses, Boy Scout activities, parades (Holiday in Dixie would incorporate beautifully with this new plan), informal concerts, an open shuttle for bus tours, sidewalk artists, sidewalk cafes, animal and pet competitions, paddleboat rentals, church services, celebrations, school promotions and graduations, election campaigns, fireworks, bicycle riding, seating/walking/resting/watching—the list and variety are endless!

In all, the Riverfront Complex encompasses the development of forty-five acres, bounded by Cross Bayou on the north, Red River on the east, I-20 on the south and Commerce Street on the west.

Why become concerned about the Red River . . . about re-developing the riverfront in general?

Because it is a vital and living reminder of our link with the past—a permanent part of our heritage—our past, our present, our future. Its potential is boundless. With re-navigation more than just a distant possibility, Big Red will once again see the kind of activity that gave Shreveport its name.

Cleaning up Big Red is a vital first step, and one which the area's citizens have already embraced. Shreveport opened a huge sewage treatment facility at Lucas in 1976 as part of a program to stop dumping raw wastes into Red River. Bossier City is now embarking on a program with the same goals. There are also projects to reduce the heavy inflow of natural chlorides from salt water springs in west Texas into the river. Four thousand tons of salt sift into the Red on an average day; these projects hope to reduce this amount by 45 percent. Reducing both pollution and natural chlorides should improve the water quality for agricultural, industrial and municipal usage.

The argument for renewal of navigation concerns more than just the city's importance as a port. The distinctive feature of water transportation has always been its low cost. For the cost of hauling such commodities as coal, gasoline, fuel oil, steel, chemicals, fertilizers, or grain one mile by railroad, they can ordinarily be hauled four miles or more by water.

A scientist for the Rand Corporation reports that, for the same tonnage carried just as far, railroads burn up three gallons of fuel for each two gallons consumed by water carriers. Less fuel consumption, of course, means less air pollution. It also means bigger supplies and lower prices for the motorist at the fuel pump.

During our past decade we have evidenced a growing concern for the environment; consider that railroads and highways preempt increasingly larger expanses of land, both agricultural and urban. The broad acreages of a single urban railroad classification yard, sometimes as large as a good-sized farm, are a case in point. The right of way for water transportation, however, is almost always a natural river.

Environmentally, river transportation is certainly one of the cleaner alternatives. But there are other environmental reasons that concern larger issues. Issues like aesthetics . . . the fresh, inviting expanse of flowing water that is a river . . . an invigorating, renewing kind of sight that enriches our lives, and our children's lives. Issues like the quality of life in Shreveport . . . and what steps we can take to preserve for our children's children the memory of a time when concrete and steel were unheard-of fantasies, when traffic meant the clipped rhythm of horses' hooves, when a trip from Shreveport to New Orleans meant the leisurely passage of several days by steamboat.

If we do not protect our links with the past now, what future people will remember why it was important?

If we do not give our children a sense of pride in their past, what pride will they have in their future?

Let us make our heritage to our descendants be one of life remembered, life preserved, life enjoyed and appreciated. And through it all, the river runs—Big Red—the thread of life that has connected our ancestors with us, and us with our descendants. The Red River: powerful, resplendent red torrent of a river that demands our attention, our respect, and our help. For the future—we cannot afford to let it down!

Bibliography

Allen, Senator James B. "Taxing Waterway Benefits: But Who are the Beneficiaries?" Pamphlet, reprinted from the Congressional Record of September 28, 1976. By National Waterways Conference, Inc., 1130 17th St. N.W., Washington, D.C.

Armstrong, Amos Lee. "When the Red Was Steamboat Alley." Shreveport Magazine, April 1966.

Barker, Olden Lee. "Red River of Louisiana—Navigation." Thesis, Department of History, University of Colorado, 1929.

Bell, Thomas Fletcher. "Red River Raft." Paper read to Louisiana Historical Society in 1884.

Carruth, Viola. *Caddo: 1000.* October, 1970. Publisher, Shreveport Magazine. Mid-South Press, Shreveport, Louisiana.

"Central Business District Riverfront Development." Plan developed by Wiener, Hill, Morgan & O'Neal, Architects and Planners, and Barras Breaux Champeaux, Architecture and City Planning. January 1975.

"Civil War Marine: A Diary of the Red River Expedition, 1864." Edited and annotated by James P. Jones and Edward F. Keuchel. Booklet, History and Museums Division, Headquarters, U.S. Marine Corps, Washington, D.C. 1975. U.S. Government Printing Office.

Crowder, Walter J. "Red River, Its Valley and Its People." Letter written May 14, 1947.

Dodson, Orland. "Invitation to Reunion: Red River Navigation." Shreveport Magazine, November 1964.

________. "Freshening Red River and the Sea of Air." Shreveport Magazine, January 1977.

________. "Pivotal April—Month of Action on the Red." Shreveport Magazine, April 1965.

Hardin, James Fair. *Northwestern Louisiana: A History of the Watershed of the Red River, 1714-1937, Volumes I-III.* The Historical Record Association, Louisville, Kentucky and Shreveport, Louisiana, 1936.

Holding, Reynolds. "Benefits Debate Muddies Red River Project." Newspaper article, *Shreveport Journal*, October 26, 1978.

________. "Elusive Red River Project." Newspaper article, *Shreveport Journal*, October 25, 1978.

Lamb, Bobby. "The Bridging of Two Cities." Newspaper article, *Shreveport Times*, March 4, 1979.

Marcy, *Adventure on Red River*, Louisiana Collection, edited by Grant Foreman, 1937, University of Oklahoma Press, Norman, Oklahoma.

O'Pry, Maude Hearn, *Chronicles of Shreveport and Caddo Parish*, 1927. (No publisher listed).

Shreveport-Bossier City Telephone Directory, January 1979. Published by South Central Bell Telephone Company.

"Status of Corps of Engineers Projects, Red River Valley." ________ booklet, December 1978.

U.S. Corps of Engineers. "Red River Waterway." Pamphlet, June 1977, New Orleans District.

Winterton, Mary Moss. "Reflections of a Rivertown." Booklet, AAA Printing, Shreveport, Louisiana, 1975. Published by Chi Omega Alumnae.

Credits

EXECUTIVE EDITOR
Doug Woolfolk
ASSOCIATE EDITOR/DESIGN
Conrad Wilson
RESEARCH AND COPY
Judy Williams
COVER DESIGN
Stan Taylor
PUBLISHING CONSULTANT
Myron Tassin

Photographs

Barksdale Museum, Barksdale A.F.B.*
Page 58.
Anthony Garner
Pages 12, 14, 15, 24, 85.
Grabill Studios, Shreveport
Pages 18, 22, 26 bottom, 27 top left, 37.
Louisiana State Library
Pages 20, 26 top, 27 top right, 28, 38, 47, 51, 54, 56.
Department of Archives and Manuscripts, Louisiana State University, Baton Rouge, Louisiana
Pages 42, 48.
Louisiana State University in Shreveport Archives
Pages 21, 33 bottom, 44.
Louisiana Office of Tourism
Pages 8, 9, 60, 75, 77, 80.
R.W. Norton Art Gallery, Shreveport (painting by Lloyd F. Hawthorne)
Page 30.
Red River Revel (photographs by Robert K. Giss)
Page 79.
Red River Valley Association
Pages 36, 53, 65, 66, 68, 73, 74.
Shreve Memorial Library
Page 32.
Shreveport Chamber of Commerce
Pages 15 top, 25 (Grabil photograph), 27 bottom.
Shreveport-Bossier Convention-Tourist Bureau
Pages 46, 63, 76, 78.
U.S. Army Corps of Engineers
Pages 31, 33 top, 39.

* Reproduction of Air Force photographs does not necessarily imply endorsement of any commercial firm.